Adversperience

The CONVERGENCE
of ADVERTISING & EXPERIENTIAL MARKETING

ISBN: 978-0-9921479-0-7

Printed in Canada.

Editing: Catherine Leek, Green Onion Publishing
Layout: Linda Alaggia, Computer Composition of Canada
Cover and Interior Design: Nicole Ruznisky
Illustrations: Nick Craine

To the Wizard in all of Us!

Dream a Little Dream ...

Dreams can come true, they can happen to you, if you are young at heart ... and that I am.

Adversperience is the beginning of a dream come true. It is the first of many books and dreams. It will hopefully put my company in the spotlight; give my team, our work, and our industry some much deserved recognition; and fulfill my dream to write, speak, and mentor/teach. All things that feed that the lives and spirits of my amazing circle of family and friends.

We live our legacy every day and writing this book tells a story itself – of overcoming personal and professional challenges, ignoring the naysayers, realizing that with a "mono-maniacal" focus fueled by relentless determination and a dream team of loving support (aka my three children), absolutely any dream can come true.

Gabe, Mariah and Gianni – you are my dream team. I am blessed every day to be your mom – you are amazing. You have supported and taught me more than a mom can ever imagine.

Gabe, you have taught me to pursue my dreams and passions irrespective of expected norms. You have patiently raised me through motherhood and loved me inspite of my foibles. Thank you for loving me when I am the most difficult to love, for listening to me rant and rave with great patience, and laughing with and at me. Thank you for getting up with me at 5 am (to realize my dreams and to write this book!) – dream team power! You have been

—— •••• ᘐ •••• ——

a great partner on so many levels, far too much responsibility for an oldest child but you wear it well.

Mariah, my beautiful and natural beach princess with such a gentle, intuitive spirit – you are the self I aspire to be. You are the wisest and most loving person. Anyone who gets to hold your hand and heart should feel blessed. I cherish time with you and thank you for always holding my hand. You fuel all those around you with the magic in your eyes and your spontaneous spirit – you are magic! Thank you for telling me I can do anything and that I am beautiful.

And my Gianni, you have proven that with focus and discipline any goal can be achieved. You gently nudge me along when the emotions and fatigue are overwhelming and hold me tight and let me cry when I am both happy and very very sad. Just your hug makes me feel better. Note the "my" Gianni, you are my protector in so many ways, hence the reason I hold on to you so tight. It is not just your stature but the warmth and charm that eminates from you that makes our entire little family feel secure in your presence. We see and feel your power and know you too are starting to see and feel it.

From all three of you I have found safety, sanctuary, unconditional love, and infinite inspiration. Thank you. We can individually and jointly achieve anything. The three of you are my greatest friends and fans. I love you.

To my mom, thank you for being there whenever you are needed, for creating a unique and special place in my heart and that of each of my children, for teaching me to get on with life when I thought the fairy tale was over, and for being living proof that even at 71 dreams can come true.

To my sister Marissa, brother-in-law Taz, and awesome nephew Carter and niece Frankie – you guys all live life every day and cherish family. I love the magic in your spirits and your home. I wish that for everyone! Marissa, I wish you the success you so greatly deserve. You are amazing – never ever doubt that. I love you.

To my team at BOOM! and specifically my "Rat Pack:" Linsey Ferguson, Bailey Dougherty, Lee McGrath, and Scott Kinnear. Look at what we've done! In the process of doing great work we have built a great company, great families, and great love.

Lins, thank you for always telling me it was going to be okay (even when we did not have a clue), for being strong when I was not, and for keeping me going. You have been balanced, clearheaded, and methodical when I and the team have needed the guidance. You have been the best "coach's coach" – every coach needs a coach and you coach with a firm hand and a very tender heart and I thank you – I love you.

Scottie, you are this burst of quirky, smart and touching sensitivity. Thank you for your decisive and gentle guiding hand on all of the design elements of the book and all our work – big things ahead. Thank you for checking in on me and keeping me steady – I love you.

LeeLee, I cannot thank you enough for your intense loyalty and love – I feel it every day and so strongly and aggressively when we are at "war." Thank you for making me feel like you have my back every day – I love you.

And Bails, you make me feel smart and wise and beautiful and important every day unconditionally – I love you. Love lives at our office and that makes it all worthwhile! Thank you BOOM! team – we are EXTRAORDINARY!

To Nicole Ruznisky, thank you for all your design ideas and support. You design with a smile and spirit that comes through in all your work.

To Nick Craine, thanks for overthinking all the design elements, for working patiently though hurriedly on the visuals that all came together at the end of the process … and you never complained and you made me rethink and clarify.

To our amazing supplier partners and clients, the warmest and sincerest of thanks. I love what I do and the people I do it with. Thank you for having and sharing the faith!

To Paul Brent, Linda Rowe, Linda Alaggia and Catherine Leek, thank you for patiently coaching me along, editing, sharing when things did not feel right, and adjusting my path along the yellow brick road. The next book should be easier!

Many years ago a very wise woman, Iris Benrubi, once said to me that people come into your life for a reason, a season, or a lifetime. The thanks below are for the "reason" people in my life.

Paul, our fairy tale did not unfold as we imagined but our children are magic and will change the world. Thank you for what we had and these three magical people we created. Buckle up world, they are coming!

Iris, you saved me on many dark, scattered, chaotic, messy days. For me, you are a magical gypsy and have been a *great* role model and mentor and a true inspiration. Thank you.

Robin Sharma, at the time of writing this we have yet to meet, which is proof that you can have a *great* impact on someone without shaking their hand. I attended T48T, a leadership development course, and since then I have shared the learnings and keep absorbing more from all your books and online teachings – thank you. You have greatly touched my spirit. I am a lifelong student and a *great* fan.

Johanne Belley, my beautiful French friend, I love you. Thanks for making me feel like my foibles are all okay and for gently being my friend and providing a gentle guiding hand when I have been lonely.

And to Bailey, Bails we trade roles–sister, mother, daughter, friend. You show up unannounced, supportive and loving when I am the least loving and messy and you still love me unconditionally and then you bring me flowers or make cookies. You are true, loyal, and loving to the core and I thank you for always providing tender healing love for my heart and soul when it has been wounded, and for jumping up and down and doing the Happy Dance with me when things are awesome, and for celebrating family every day. And Justin, thanks for being Bailey's amazing husband and making me feel like I am "hot" and that one day I will find that "lucky guy."

Alyssa Bodrug, you are a magical spirit met through a friend at work and now you are so intertwined into the spiritual beliefs that ground our hearts and our home that we look forward to seeing you at every visit and cherish time with you. You are beyond special to my children and I – thank you.

To all of you with this book in your hand, thank you for flipping through the pages. That in itself is the greatest reward.

This is a dream come true. See you soon in The Emerald City.

Thank you,
Nicole

—···· χ ····—

CONTENTS

CONTENTS

JOIN US in the EMERALD CITY

There has been talk of purple cows and flying fish, six thinking hats, the one-to-one consumer and the power of now ... all good, all true. This book is not those.

This book contains fact-based learning from the marketing world today balanced with whimsy which is the creative magic that our industry is known for, inspired by *The Wizard of Oz*. This book confidently makes a point and humbly takes a stand.

Adversperience is about what the consumer "senses." This book integrates purple cow strategy, stimulated by thinking hats, from an organization that embraces flying fish and thrives on motivating each other with compassion and a respect for the challenges of life to ensure that we live our best lives and do our best work every day in the competency of our choice. In the case of myself and my team, that is Experiential Marketing.

The visual of the little man hiding behind the curtain declaring that he is the Great and Terrible Oz brings to mind some self-doubt as I write this book. My two demons/wicked Witches of the West cause me to worry that:

1. I have no right to write this book.

2. I am dropping a bomb on the advertising and marketing world.

Please bear with me and let's tackle my first point. I'm fairly well known in the Canadian Experiential Marketing world and my agency has won a few worldwide awards, but I am hardly famous. You will not confuse me with David Ogilvy or Lee Clow, legends in the advertising world. Do you need to be an advertising legend to write a book on the future of advertising as converging with the tactic Experiential Marketing? Do you need to be famous to write a business book? No!

In the end, the content and thoughts you bring forward determine your success. Experiential Marketing is the redheaded stepchild of advertising. I hope I have and will continue to prove to you that it shouldn't be and will not be for much longer. All modesty aside, I have as much "right" to write this book as anyone else in this business.

I have been around the marketing world for three decades (*ugh!*). I read, research, and devour reports and books on the latest and greatest. I have built budgets, brands, strategies, and thankfully won more competitive battles than I have lost. I have been client side, agency side, and straddled both worlds for eight years as I ran my own "new product launch" consulting/project management agency. So, I have some thoughts, I have backed them up with research and if you agree or disagree – awesome. Let's have the conversation.

As for the bomb – let's be honest, it's ticking away in virtually every company's marketing department and in all marketing agencies, regardless of competency. There is no sure footing, everything is changing by the minute, and the stuff that used to work so well, mass media using print, TV, and even some online, just isn't going to cut it today and especially tomorrow.

Target markets are digitally distracted and hyper-connected to the point that most conventional advertising is either being missed or completely unnoticed. That's why Experiential Marketing, and especially Adversperiential Marketing (happening though unlabeled till now!) is making inroads. For the first few chapters, I continue to use the term "Experiential" as until now that is what everyone has been familiar with. That said, please know by the end of this book my expectation is that we will have aligned on the merits, coined a new term, and you will join me in using it as we move forward. Truth is, it's happening, I just gave it a name.

So here is some truth, justified after having attended yet another marketing awards gala. There were a multitude of categories and in most cases "Ad" agencies took the top prize. The most interesting point though is that every single award – and I mean every single one – included or was driven by Experiential Marketing. Advertising agencies are embracing Experiential Marketing because traditional methods and media are not breaking through the clutter. Adversperiential campaigns are breaking through – advertising that can be experienced and then as a result often goes "viral" thanks to word of mouth online and off. Adversperiential campaigns took the top prizes in every category! Proof positive that Adversperiential Marketing is here.

This likely makes everyone uncomfortable. Change often does. At our agency we live outside of our comfort zone – pretty much every day. We never do anything twice and we fret over the smallest of details.

I say that because Experiential Marketing is a tough industry. Because an Adversperience is live you have to be on 24/7 and that is a different way of working – it takes a special breed of smart and crazy!

This book is about the learnings of a great team in a rapidly moving and changing industry and our efforts to build brands and impact consumers.

There has been an attempt to avoid rhetoric and identify facts whenever and wherever possible. That said, I am a marketer to the core and marketing is a combination of art and science – greatness happens when common sense simplicity prevails.

Adversperience is our methodical perspective on building brands. In our very humble opinion, the core principles for building brands is very much the same as it has been since the beginning of time – create a solid product/service that has a relevant need, give it a name, get it out for the target to try, develop awareness, and build lifetime loyalty. Okay, I have oversimplified it, but I trust you get the point. While building brands has not changed, the world in which we are building them changes by the nanosecond. The communication and impulses around us to try the "Ultra, Super, Shiny, New" are absolutely everywhere.

Adversperience – a term we coined – is our take on how brands can relevantly reach and touch consumer senses and get noticed in this 21st century of distraction, mass proliferation, and global connection!

Adversperience is the convergence of advertising and experiential marketing – it is live, participatory advertising. Consumers and key stakeholders are engaged and involved in a brand experience that touches many of their senses. This is evolutionary thinking that is stirring a revolution.

Hopefully as you read along you will laugh, smile, and the thought lines between your eyebrows will furl (*yup, that's a word*). The intent in sharing is to provide an enjoyable and thought-provoking read and spread the Adversperiential word. To join the conversation or participate in the revolution, please connect to us at *Adversperience.com.*

So, where to from here? Well, the foundation is shaking and the cyclone is all around us. Hold my hand, we are heading in ...

Chapter 1

The Cyclone

The Story of Experiential Marketing

"There is no place like home."

nce upon a time ... yadda, yadda, yadda ... and they lived happily ever after. Isn't this how we would like every book, every story, every life to go?

Not so sure this is the right way to begin a business book and yet in the marketing world to start the first chapter of a book similar to the way a fairy tale begins seems on point! This story is a journey. We have been swooped up in a cyclone of distraction, disruption, and chaos and in an attempt to find sure ground we are tenuously traveling along a yellow brick road to a magical wizard in a land of hopeful riches. Beginning with once-upon-a-time seems to make the marketing cyclone of the moment less scary!

Pre-cyclone or in more settled "once upon a times," Experiential Marketing was a key character in any brand marketing fairy tale, like the Tin Woodman, for instance. Rarely was it the Wizard, never the Wicked Witch, on the odd occasion it was Glinda, the Good Witch. But in this story we'll show that it has always played the role of Dorothy – leading the charge, winning the battles, enduring life and limb and prevailing, though often without the fanfare or accolades so many of its peers require. In fact, we'll prove that Experiential Marketing successes – short and long term – are often greater and certainly more enduring than those of its peers.

Experiential Marketing knows that the odd challenge may be lost but the greater goal is to get home to Kansas or an Emerald City of our design – and that it has!

However, *The Wizard of Oz* was written at the turn of the last century and, like all such stories, much has changed. The 21st century is an age of distraction, and will see two characters joining forces and morphing into a Marketing Superpower – and that is Adversperiential Marketing. Advertising and Experiential Marketing will join forces and through astute planning will reign supreme and brands will flock to their feet in order to gain recognition among the global masses. Adversperience is the new and all powerful Wizard and it lives confidently and humbly in The Emerald City. You are welcome to visit, just follow the yellow brick road.

The goal of this book is to take you along the journey, the yellow brick road, to successfully market products and services to defined target markets with a specific focus in one area – Experiential Marketing with the evolution to Adversperiential Marketing.

The Evolution to Adversperiential Marketing

Experiential Marketing is a live, two-way engagement between brands and their target. Done right it is authentic/real, achieves the objectives of trial and awareness, and creates a long-term and more loyal consumer.

Marketing as a whole is changing daily thanks to continuous communication in an ever-connected global community. According to research, people spend 2.1 hours every day in distraction at work. In fact, every 11 minutes we are being distracted and it then takes 25 minutes to refocus. Rarely do we ever focus uninterrupted for a period of time. What is distracting us is human connection – real or online – live conversations or chats on Twitter, facebook, you name it. Constant is the need for human connection, regardless of time, space, tactics, methodologies, or technologies. As marketers our goal is to build a brand connection. This is most effectively done through experiences and engagements that are relevant and resonate not only in the moment but over time (delivering lifetime value).

Brands today live in a cluttered world so how can they resonate with consumers, build a connection? The truth is that everyone is asking this question and yet the answer remains simplistically the same – brands need to reach out and "touch" their consumers – physically, mentally, spiritually (*I can imagine a few eyes rolling as I make that statement – but it's true – look at your own connections in life – the strongest ones connect with you on multiple levels*). As opposed to all other marketing tactics, Experiential Marketing is the only tactic that can achieve the goal of "touch." Experiential marketing can reach out and touch several senses simultaneously – this is its magic versus any other tactic available to marketers. That said, it too is growing and changing as are all marketing disciplines. Really, Experiential Marketing is evolving into its truer self – Adversperiential Marketing.

A bunch of kids standing on a street corner handing out product samples is *not* a good example of Experiential Marketing. Experiential Marketing done well is brand theater, it is the brand advertising – everything a commercial wants to say, do, demonstrate, brought to life and wrapped in a story that is relevant to the consumer and will continue to resonate long after the experience is over.

When we founded our company, the inclusion of quotes to accompany each person's signature was a defining attribute of our culture. Our quotes are very personal and speak about what each of us deems to be important in the world of Experiential Marketing. My quote, "Nothing is ever real until it is experienced," is from Gilmore and Pine's book *The Experience Economy* and is a timeless quote, relevant for life. We don't really "know" until we experience. True of life, love, work, pain, joy, ... the list goes on. We don't know, until we know! I have been saying this in various ways for years, as have others before me, such as Drucker with his theories on the lifetime value of the consumer and Peppers and Rogers who in 1993 wrote *The One to One Future: Building Relationships One Customer at a Time* with principles for building brands that are as true today as they were then. My point is that while much has changed, much remains the same. We are distracted more than ever. A new generation of technology is presented to us before we are even familiar with the previous. But what has not changed is the way we connect to each other and build relationships. Life is faster but it is still life!

Clutter and busyness are not new topics that impact a brand being heard. It's the speed and magnitude of the clutter and busyness that is the increasing challenge. What has changed in the past 20+ years is the context for the conversation. Twenty-five years ago, the premise behind the value of one-to-one marketing was heavily weighted in the need to gain lifelong consumers for various products and brands. Keep in mind that at this time the average grocery store carried 20,000 skus, there were 30-40 TV channels, a similar number of radio stations, and land line telephones! Today stores carry over 80,000 skus, there are over 3 million consumer brands, and consumers are daily inundated with over 3,000 different messages. Proliferation and clutter are the order of the day.

In the 1950s, 60s, 70s, 80s, 90s, an ad would run on television one day and sales would be up the next day. The impact was immediate. Those in the marketing world embraced advertising and reveled in the glory that the simplest messaging outlining their product's unique selling proposition (USP) would drive brand sales within days. As the complexity of advertising and media grew, so too did brand creativity. "Breakthrough" ads with "big ideas" that "disrupt" became the objective of everyone in the industry. As competition grew more fierce, messaging proliferated, the noise and volume increased and continues to increase. So how do brands win?

With the turn of the century came the rise in Experiential Marketing – getting the right product directly into the hands of the right consumer in a place, at a time, and with key messaging/staging that is relevant, resonates, and is memorable and firmly entrenches the brand in the consumer's heart and mind. And like other tactics, Experiential Marketing continues to evolve ... Adversperience.

The dawn of Adversperiential Marketing is upon us – and once again brand marketers must seize the opportunity to influence consumers or perish!

Some History for Perspective

By our very human nature, we have evolved through stories. Cave man drew pictures on walls to communicate. There were circles around firepits and campfires and today we sit around kitchen tables to share stories and solve problems. Storytelling has been and always will be critical to our lives and evolution – it's how we make decisions for living (the choice for a holiday is most often due to a conversation among friends) and also the legacy we leave (note a Coca-Cola case study about a vending machine that unites India and Pakistan that will be discussed later).

AD Age produced a timeline covering a century of advertising. The first newspaper advertisement, an announcement seeking a buyer for an Oyster Bay, Long Island, estate, was published in the *Boston News-Letter*. Benjamin Franklin began publishing the *Pennsylvania Gazette* in Philadelphia, which included pages of "new advertisements." This thinking gave birth to the model of lowering newspaper prices, extending readership, and increasing profitability – a model soon copied by other newspapers. Around 1840, Volney B. Palmer established the roots of the modern-day advertising agency in Philadelphia. In 1842 Palmer bought large amounts of space in various newspapers at a discounted rate then resold the space at higher rates to advertisers.

At the time Palmer was a space-broker – he pioneered media buying. At this time, brands created their own ads but he soon realized this was not their competency and he provided "creative" services to round out his offerings. And the rest shall we boldly say is history ... with the invention of radio, came the first radio ad in 1922; and with the invention of TV, came the first TV ad in 1941.

Fast forward to today, and countless "inventions" to satisfy humans' insatiable appetite for new and improved.

Today "there are over 3,200,000,000 likes and comments every day. That's 3.2 billion! Or 37,000 every second." (Source: Facebook 2012). If Facebook was a continent, it would be the second largest, closing the gap to be the largest within the next year? And annual global advertising spending is at $557 billion.

Clearly what worked in 1836 no longer works in the 21st century. When the first TV ads were launched, sales were literally impacted within 24-48 hours.

Today, "only 47% of consumers around the world say they trust paid media (television, magazine, radio and newspaper ads), a decline of over 20% since 2009." (Source: Nielsen, April 2012)

> In the last few years, the web has started living up to its oft-discussed potential for becoming the most exciting playground in advertising. A significant reason, we think, is drawn from two attributes of online media; sharing is central, and the interface can be customized.

Sharing is an obvious one…no other advertising format – television, print, radio or outdoor – can so easily and instantly be shared as the URL. Online content lives or dies depending on whether or not it's passed around. There is just too much information out there for this not to be the case.

(Source: Aaron Koblin (Creative Director, Google Creative Lab) and Valdean Klump (Copywriter, Google Creative Lab), *Game Changers, The Evolution of Advertising*, p. 243)

By the second decade of the 21st century, the average person is now spending 30 minutes to an hour a day online. With a huge percentage of that time spent on mobile devices, the term "the always-on consumer" may have been an exaggeration, but only a mild one.

Just as the cultural revolution of the 1960s blurred the boundaries between literature, music, art, and entertainment, so the technology revolution is blurring distinctions between products to the point where they are no longer useful or relevant. Is a bank now a building or an app? Is a phone a phone or is it a computer? (Source: *Game Changers*, p. 281)

And it all started with the simple insight that technology can play a role in transforming people's lives, not just delivering another campaign message. (Source: *Game Changers*, p. 289 per Bob Greenberg, Chairman and CEO, R/GA)

Reflective of our changing media consumption patterns (witness 37,000 likes per second) are changing patterns of consumer trust/receptivity to messages – "92% of global consumers say they trust earned media (word of mouth and recommendations), above all other forms of advertising resulting in an increase of 18% since 2007." (Source: Nielsen, April 2012)

While some things have changed, some things remain the same. People, their experiences, and the stories they tell as a result remain the most powerful medium.

As this first chapter comes to a close I hope I have made the point that advertising is extremely important and the need to bring it to life increasingly critical in this cyclone-like age of disruption and distraction. We will go on to prove that just as advertising has evolved so has Experiential Marketing. It has become more than the "below-the-line tactic" it was relegated to in historical marketing budgets. In this century, and even more so in this decade, the two – Advertising and Experiential Marketing – will converge in order to gain the ever distracted attention of their target. Adversperiential Marketing will become the new norm.

Critical to writing this book was ensuring I had cases studies, facts, and live examples that demonstrate what, why, and how. In so doing, I talked to marketers, researchers, read books, surfed the net, and just as I was knee deep I hopped on a plane and headed to the 60th Annual Lions Cannes Festival of Creativity. (*As an aside if you have not been – GO!*) You will see many learnings from the Festival throughout the book. On June 20, 2013, midway through the Festival, Cirque du Soleil and Sid Lee announced a joint venture to form Sid Lee

Entertainment. "The new company will develop and implement innovative and unique entertainment platforms for advertisers in order for the consumer to live an experience closely linked to the brand's attributes." Daniel Lamarre, Cirque du Soleil's President and CEO declared, "Through Sid Lee Entertainment, Cirque du Soleil wishes to use their expertise to serve advertisers with the creation of new platforms which will be specifically developed to bring their brand DNA to life."

An advertising agency partnering with the world's most extraordinary theatrical performance circus to create campaigns for brands to engage their target – this is proof positive that we are not in Kansas anymore and while the cyclone may be scary, we are in it. It's powerful, colourful and magical and there is a "light at the end of the tunnel." Just follow the yellow brick road ...

As we head into Adversperience, this is a good place to get really specific and provide some definitions of terms.

According to the Oxford Dictionary:

Advertising: *(noun)* The activity or profession of producing advertisements for commercial products or services: *movie audiences are receptive to advertising (as modifier) an advertising agency*

Marketing: *(noun)* The action or business of promoting and selling products or services, including market research and advertising.

According to Industry Consensus:

Experiential Marketing: Relevant live engagement between brands and their target consumer with the intent to create lasting, memorable, and measurable impressions online and offline.

According to Nicole Gallucci and subscribers to the revolution

Adversperiential Marketing: The convergence of advertising and experiential marketing.

Live sensory-driven brand engagements designed to communicate brand USP and story in a way that is relevant and resonates with the target consumer to the point that they not only become loyal users but also ambassadors. Connection to the brand builds before there is a launch/crescendo which is the point when the target is engaged on a multisensory level. Relevantly engaged, the consumer and brand stay connected enhancing loyalty and promoting social conversation online and off until the next crescendo. Adversperiential Marketing is a continuum of multisensory engagement.

In the spirit of "let's get at it" we hope you enjoy *Adversperience!*

Chapter 2

Finding Solid Ground in Oz

The IMPACT of EXPERIENTIAL MARKETING

*The cyclone had set the house down very gently –
for a cyclone – in the midst of a country of marvelous beauty.*

...

*"You are welcome, most noble Sorceress, to the land
of the Munchkins. We are so grateful to you for having
killed the Wicked Witch of the East, and for
setting our people free from bondage."*

ost people have heard the famous phrase, "It was the best of times, it was the worst of times ..." It is the opening line from Charles Dickens' *Tale of Two Cities* (based on France and England circa 1775). Few know the lines that follow. "[I]t was the age of wisdom, it was the age of foolishness, it was the epoch of belief, it was the epoch of incredulity, it was the season of Light, it was the season of Darkness, it was the spring of hope, it was the winter of despair ..."

That pretty much sums up the world of marketing today that makes me feel like we are in a whirling cyclone. Plenty of hope and promise that tools and techniques are getting better and better and constant worry that the old ways of marketing simply do not work anymore. Truth is the laws of attraction remain but the laws of distraction rule the land!

The Best and Worst of Marketing Times

The first newspaper ad appeared in 1704, the first radio in 1922, and the first TV ad aired in 1941. In each case the impact was revolutionary and the face of marketing was forever changed. In the 60s case studies consistently proved that if you aired a TV ad, sales were impacted the next day. In the 80s, as a Brand Manager at Nestle, I would buy sufficient media to ensure that the target consumer saw our commercial a minimum of eight times.

Studies proved that if a consumer saw our ad eight times then our "awareness" would be strong enough that they would then purchase our product. People would walk along the street singing ad jingles and taglines would frequently be part of conversations. There was association – "plop, plop, fizz fizz, oh what a relief it is" (Alka Seltzer) – connection – "I'd like to teach the world to sing" (Coca-Cola) – and resonance – "good to the last drop" (Maxwell House). People got it and bought it! Market share was truly won and lost based on how compelling your ads were. Consumers would try your product and if it delivered, then they were loyal. It was the best of times!

Then times changed and with each advancement there was commoditization of the goods and services that preceded the latest and greatest version. Brands and consumer expectations rose. There was constant need for "new" and "improved." And while brands proliferated so too did media modes and methods. More … more … more has become the order of the day. Today in my grocery store I noted eight different formats and/or types of eggs – eight! As with the increased availability of goods and services there has been commoditization. Commoditization, mass proliferation, and mass distraction. It is the worst of times!

That said, the old laws of attraction remain and the "Super, Shiny, New, Improved" widgets and wonders are continuously being sought and launched. We need to accept and harness distraction and disruption. It is the dawn of new times!

Consumers – "beings" we at one time called "people" – are using and being used minute by minute by media and communication and technology. Most carry around digital devices with awesome power to make their lives easier and more complicated – and much, much more distracted. So marketers attempt to compete by the same rules.

Campaigns that distract and/or disrupt proliferate – some win, some lose. The difference resides in understanding the consumer (queue rolling eyes, *nothing new here*). But I mean *truly* understand. Society is fragmented and we need to understand consumers extraordinarily well so that we can find that one nugget, that one needle in the haystack of information that will pave our way into their hearts, minds, and pockets.

The Facts Speak

In order to understand and therefore embrace the relevance and impact of Experiential Marketing and its evolution to Adversperiential Marketing we need to look at some facts (*I know, yet another pie chart*). As marketers trying to get the latest and greatest brand through the distraction barrier, we need to understand what is effective and reaches consumers.

Media Consumption

First let's look at a few facts about how consumers take in media. (Source: The Brand Builder, blog by Olivier Blanchard, November 2, 2012)

The volume of global media consumption doubles every 25 years or so. And this does not take into consideration multiple screens – two and three at a time. The biggest change occurred in 2007, when 50% of media was digital. By 2020, it is predicted that 80% of media will be digital.

Here are some quick facts about media types and formats.

- Print is decreasing and it has been since the dawn of TV. Pre-TV, print boasted 90-100% of media dollars.

- Analog TV and radio have been replaced by digital.

- Radio continues to be flat.

- TV experienced huge growth from 1940 to 1980, but has been relatively flat since then. (NOTE: The graph in Exhibit 2.1 does not include channel proliferation and fragmentation, but consumption only. Therefore, if you are doing the math on the impact of consumption, it is flat or down but the volume of choice is up so the impact on the "value" of your buy (*ugh – now we can all shrug/roll our eyeballs!*).

- Outdoor has been relatively flat, as has cinema.

- So, what's growing? Da da da daaaaa! ... Internet/ digital, mobile, games ... shocking! (*yes, read with sarcasm*)

Exhibit 2.1
How Do We Consume Media?

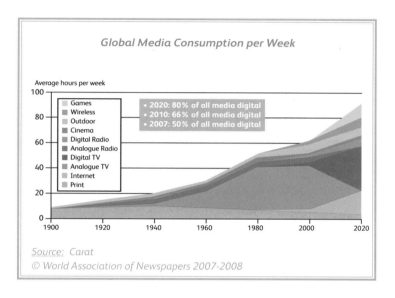

Global Media Consumption per Week

Average hours per week

Legend:
- Games
- Wireless
- Outdoor
- Cinema
- Digital Radio
- Analogue Radio
- Digital TV
- Analogue TV
- Internet
- Print

- 2020: 80% of all media digital
- 2010: 66% of all media digital
- 2007: 50% of all media digital

Source: Carat
© World Association of Newspapers 2007-2008

The point of it all is that brands need to say, "Hello, how are you? It's really great to meet you. Can we chat?" And nothing, absolutely nothing, can do this like Experiential Marketing. And I will reiterate that successful, effective Experiential Marketing is Adversperiential!

Read on!!!!!

It is one thing to say something works and another thing to prove it. Some qualitative facts will demonstrate successes.

Qualitative Facts

Experiences resonate. This is true in life and in marketing. We mark out life by milestones – first kiss, driver's license, graduation, marriage, birth of children, first house, first car … and the list goes on.

Experiences also resonate in our brain. They withstand the test of time.

Let's follow the path – the yellow brick road if you will – of Experiential Marketing. There are four facts, as solid as the bricks in the road.

1. Experiential Marketing drives purchases.

2. Events provide testing that drives the inclination to purchase.

3. Experiential Marketing builds repeat consumption and loyalty.

4. They tell others!

1. Drives the Purchase

For over 20 years, Experiential Marketing has been consistent in driving consumers to try and to buy more than any other tactic. In 52% of the cases it influences consumers to at least try a new or different product.

#1 in Driving Purchase

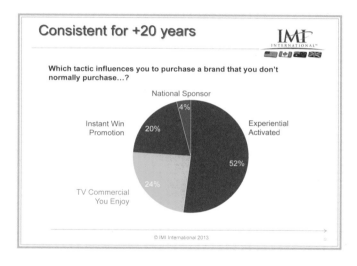

The next obvious question is why? Follow the yellow brick road to point 2.

2. Inclination to Purchase

From the start, simply attending an event makes consumers more inclined to purchase – by a whopping 95%.

Attendance Drives Inclination to Purchase

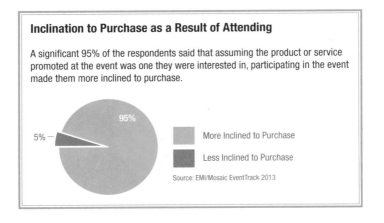

Inclination to Purchase as a Result of Attending

A significant 95% of the respondents said that assuming the product or service promoted at the event was one they were interested in, participating in the event made them more inclined to purchase.

95%

5% —

More Inclined to Purchase

Less Inclined to Purchase

Source: EMI/Mosaic EventTrack 2013

Experiential Marketing drives purchasing better than any other tactic because it has a conversation with consumers. It allows them to see and ponder before they purchase. Once influenced and engaged, it makes obvious sense that the consumer is then predisposed to try the product. And then the beauty of it all is that once the consumer tries it, they are more likely to buy!

Trials Drive Inclination to Purchase

Why More Inclined to Purchase?

Comparing two years of survey data suggests learning about benefits is becoming more important to consumers and that coupons and special offers while important, may be becoming less critical. The top response to this question in both surveys was "(the event) gave me the opportunity to try it out first" selected by 72% of the consumers in both years. In general, all of these purchase motivation factors are more important to female consumers except for "(the event) made me feel good about the product."

	2012 %	2013 %
Gave me the opportunity to try it first	72%	72%
The event/activity helped me realize I'd like or benefit from the product/event	42%	47%
I was given a discount coupon or special offer that made me more likely to buy	44%	40%
Showed that the company believed enough in its product or service to let me check it out	41%	39%
Made me feel good about the product	27%	27%
Other	2%	1%

Source: EMI/Mosaic EventTrack 2013

3. Builds Retention and Loyalty

Experiential Marketing has long been noted as building loyalty and value better than any other tactic.

Fifty-four percent of consumers said they purchased the product or service after the event, at a later date. (Follow the yellow brick road!)

Increases Purchasing Probability

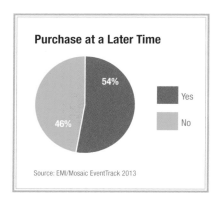

Purchase at a Later Time

54%

46%

Yes

No

Source: EMI/Mosaic EventTrack 2013

Fifty-one percent of consumers also purchased the product or service again, and a significant 88% became regular customers. Breaking out the findings by gender demonstrates that 91% of males say they then become regular customers. Fifty-five percent of females said they purchased again after the first time compared to 47% of the males. Those in the 36 to 45 and 46 to 55 age ranges are the most likely to purchase again.

Repeat Purchases

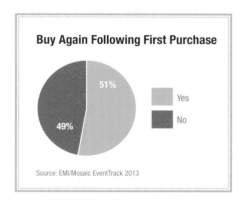

Buy Again Following First Purchase

51%

49%

Yes

No

Source: EMI/Mosaic EventTrack 2013

And once tried, they become committed and loyal customers – at least until the *Super, Shiny,* and *New* version of your product, or your competitor's, enters the clutter and shakes things up ... again! That said, done right you can hold on to your consumer if you share new developments and innovations with them ahead of all others and, even better, invite them to participate in the process.

Loyal Customers

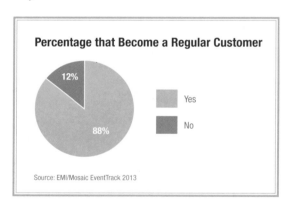

4. They Tell Others!

During the process, if the experience resonated with consumers, meaning it impacted them (we discuss this in detail in a later chapter), they'll tell others – friends, family, colleagues – and so on and so on and so on.

Telling Others

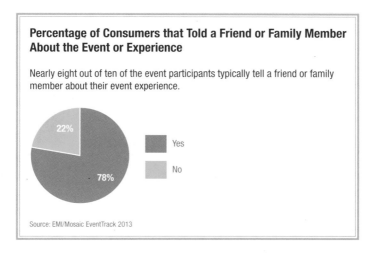

Percentage of Consumers that Told a Friend or Family Member About the Event or Experience

Nearly eight out of ten of the event participants typically tell a friend or family member about their event experience.

22%

78%

Yes

No

Source: EMI/Mosaic EventTrack 2013

If you've been following along the yellow brick road, then you've seen the signposts along the way.

1. A consumer attends an event.

2. They try/consider a product, which allows them to engage and see if/how it fits into their life.

3. They purchase it and if the product delivers, they purchase again and again.

4. If the experience resonated, then they tell others.

What Do the Facts Tell Us?

With some help from *blackcoffee.com* let me draw some conclusions. (Source: *blackcoffee.com/brand-related/brand- articles/ what-is-branding*).

A brand is like a trademark. It can be defined as a name, sign, symbol, device, or a combination thereof, intended to identify and differentiate the goods and services of one seller from those of other sellers, or group of sellers, within the same category.

From a business perspective a brand is a tool by which the company promotes goods and services to secure future earnings. As viewed by consumers a brand is the promise and delivery of an experience throughout every point of contact.

Companies create campaigns as a means of defining their brands in the minds of consumers. Ideally the campaign explains its unique selling proposition (USP) – what it stands for – often leveraging association from other things (causes, sponsorships, etc.) or people (celebrity endorsements or visuals that depict the ideal user) in order to clarify who should use the brand and why.

In practice, a brand is an experience living at the intersection of promise and expectation. Messaging needs to have a multitude of elements and be in a multitude of formats in order to break through an overcrowded marketplace.

Consumers use brands as a method for navigating their way through the marketplace. When brand meaning and relevance are clear, the brand will hold a stronger position in a consumer's mind, making them more likely to choose it. With overcrowding of not only brands but also the means to connect to the consumer, the consumer is overwhelmed and so it is increasingly critical that we connect with them on a multitude of sensory levels interactively – hence Experiential Marketing.

We have proven in this chapter that Experiential Marketing works. We all know the importance of brands. The next step is accepting that we are the most distracted species to date and this is only going to continue. To reach consumers we must stop them in their tracks with relevant marketing efforts that matter and differentiate brands and that can only truly be achieved with an Adversperience!

No other strategy or tactic is this powerful.

To fully understand, balance, and optimize this power requires intimate knowledge of the characters to whom we want to connect and the magic we need to invoke to inspire them … along the yellow brick road we go.

"The thinking that we are has brought us
to where we have already been. In order to go
somewhere else, we must think in a different way."
Albert Einstein

Chapter 3

What or Who is Oz?

WHO is the CONSUMER?

"I thought Oz was a great Head," said Dorothy.
"And I thought Oz was a lovely Lady," said the Scarecrow.
"And I thought Oz was a terrible Beast," said the Tin Woodman.
"And I thought Oz was a Ball of Fire," exclaimed the Lion.

s in most fairy tales, in the Land of Oz there is a cast of characters: there are the hero and heroine – Dorothy, the great and terrible Oz, and Glinda the Good Witch; the sidekicks – the Scarecrow, Tin Woodman and Lion; and minor charcters of interest – the Munchkins and winged monkeys; and, of course, the villain – the Wicked Witch of the West. Regardless there is someone who at the end of the day rules the land. In the case of *The Wizard of Oz,* it was the Wizard himself. Of note though is that everyone had a different impression of Oz – what or who he is/was. There are many parallels here with marketing and trying to understand who the consumer really is.

In the case of marketing, there are many rulers – clients, agencies, brands, suppliers, the almighty dollar, but I digress! All joking aside there is a constant battle in the land of marketing over who will reign supreme – the "shopper" or the "consumer?"

This is not an easy question to answer and in the world of Experiential and Adversperiential Marketing, it is *fundamental* to the experience that we create – *absolutely fundamental!*

Actual Consumer/Shopper Perspectives

Now we are getting into the methods to our madness. Before we get into the methodical conversation and develop a strategy, let's consider some more facts.

Nine percent of shoppers said they were satisfied with their perishable food outlet, and the trends by category were not much better (see Exhibit 3.1). This means 91% are dissatisfied. That is alarming!

Exhibit 3.1
Can't Get No Satisfaction

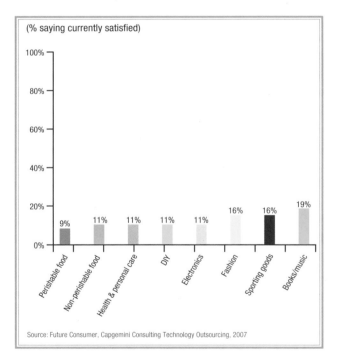

(% saying currently satisfied)

Source: Future Consumer, Capgemini Consulting Technology Outsourcing, 2007

As we develop plans to reach target audiences, we need to consider current consumer shopping patterns and trends and how these impact the campaign.

- Brands need to reconsider the traditional "path to purchase." Research now indicates that consumers make over 40% of their purchase decisions out of store. (Source: 2009 GMA)

- Add this to the dissatisfaction rates in Exhibit 3.1, and it is likely that this will lead to the already growing trend in online shopping, where consumer convenience and often price are an advantage.

- Online shopping allows for personalization, which consumers prefer. Brands will design offers specifically for their users.

- Shoppers 40+ will adjust to shifting "outlet" patterns, but the children and teens of today will be the adults and shoppers of tomorrow. They live in an online world and take for granted online research, ordering, shopping, shipping, etc. This is all part of their vernacular. Online will grow even more (see Exhibit 3.2).

- This growth in online shopping will in turn stimulate growth in other delivery systems. (We may even see a return in the importance of postal workers!) Retailers will need to find fast and efficient ways to get their products to consumers.

- In addition, with all orders and deliveries will come vertically and horizontally integrated product and service recommendations. For example, you may buy a beginner guitar, and accompanying your purchase are online and offline resources for lessons. A few quick questions to the purchaser or intuitive thinking on the part of the seller and the opportunity to customize and further support the consumer provides insane opportunities!

Exhibit 3.2
Future Change in Channel Mix

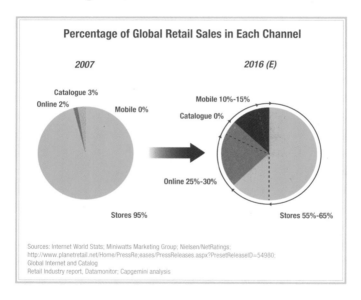

Percentage of Global Retail Sales in Each Channel

2007

Catalogue 3%
Online 2%
Mobile 0%
Stores 95%

2016 (E)

Mobile 10%-15%
Catalogue 0%
Online 25%-30%
Stores 55%-65%

Sources: Internet World Stats; Miniwatts Marketing Group; Nielsen/NetRatings;
http://www.planetretail.net/Home/PressReleases/PressReleases.aspx?PresetReleaseID=54980;
Global Internet and Catalog
Retail Industry report, Datamonitor; Capgemini analysis

Taking all the above into consideration, it begs the following question: "To whom do we market?"

Who is the Lead Character – the Shopper or the Consumer?

The discussion about "consumers" requires a slight pause – a musical interlude or intermission if you will – because we all need to take this more seriously than we do. Amidst the data tables and details on demographics and psychographics, the discussion invariably turns to whether the target group is comprised of shoppers or consumers. Who is the key? It's not just semantics, but rather a critical point.

I trust many of you are more than familiar with the rise in "Shopper Marketing," even if you are unclear of the specifics. In the spirit of keeping it simple and leaving Shopper Marketing for the experts in that practice, the key difference between a consumer and a shopper is that a "consumer" uses the product. A "shopper" buys the product. Sometimes they are the same person but not necessarily.

For example, a man (aka "the consumer") typically shaves every day. He uses or consumes products to carry out this daily ritual (razor, shaving cream, maybe aftershave). His partner (aka "the shopper") is heading to the store to grab a few things, including shaving supplies. The partner, the shopper, is told what to buy but may or may not use the product. In the case of this example, the partner in all likelihood is not using the product and has no brand preferences. In an opposing example, the partner may not have been given direction and may just buy for their consumer based on their own criteria. This scenario presents the dilemma of shopper versus consumer.

I trust it is apparent that it is the consumer who is key. In the future, the distinction between the two will likely become non-existent. The only real case where the shopper and the consumer will be evaluated and marketed to separately is in the case of small children or people for whom shopping is done without their involvement in "the grocery list."

As it relates to Experiential Marketing – evolved and improved to Adversperiential Marketing – it is even more critical we get to the consumer. We will be polite and pay our respects to shoppers in situations where there is an overlap (as noted above), but at the end of the day the Consumer is King!

Agree or disagree, I trust we are all on the same page in terms of understanding that as we move forward through this book, the focus is on the consumer with respectful nods to shoppers should they be required.

The Best Strategy to Reach Consumers

When working with clients – once we get past the objectives of trial and awareness – we get knee deep into roll-up-your sleeves conversations about their target consumer: who they are, where they live, what they eat, where they shop, their passions.

In the previous chapter we proved the value of Experiential Marketing. Yet, why do so many of us still struggle with investing dollars in this strategy?

Experiential Marketing is the Rodney Dangerfield of the marketing world. It doesn't get the respect, or the attention, that it deserves. Mostly because it is viewed as a "below the line" component of the advertising mix and therefore not considered a "strategic spend." But as we will continue to prove in this book, Experiential Marketing is by far one of the best, if not *the* best tactic, for marketers to reach consumers and gain their lifetime loyalty.

For a moment, consider your own consumer behavior. When you see your friends or colleagues on Monday morning, the first topic of conversation is "How was your weekend? What did you do?" and the conversation unfolds from there. It is the stories about what we did that are the topic: kids, family events, entertainment, perhaps shopping. Now just imagine if your brand was the main character in the story – look at the impact that your brand would have had. Perhaps one of your friends/colleagues was at an event that featured a product experience. There's a good chance that if this sort of discussion is part of a Monday morning catch-up session, word will spread about your product.

I know you all get the power of Experiential Marketing, so why the push back? Those of us in the business know the answer. The short-term return on investment (ROI) or cost per interaction/sample is higher than you would like.

The Best Payback

Experiential Marketing is constantly measured by clients and would-be clients against the cost per thousand metrics of traditional advertising. It's the wrong way to look at Experiential Marketing. Instead, what is the cost of a memorable handshake that could change your life? When you met the boss you admire most or the person you fell in love with, did this not start with a simple interaction? Hmm, are there not some parallels? I think so!

And what is the Experiential Marketing value equation? Well consider these scenarios. You spend money on a TV ad and pray that consumers see it. When consumers shake hands or make eye contact and have a conversation about your brand during an Adversperience, you don't need to pray!

And when executed effectively (more on that a bit later) your prayers are answered over and over and over. Because, as we saw in Chapter 2, once they are impacted, they buy, and, assuming the product delivers, they become loyal users.

Back to the issue of cost with regards to Experiential Marketing. A common rule of thumb is $1.00-$2.00 for each sample that is put in a consumer's hands. Often, however, we have been able to sample for pennies a piece. It all depends on traffic at the event, cost of goods for clients, and the type of event being held.

Regardless of the cost, the value of one eyeball-to-eyeball interaction far outweighs the 30-second TV spot or

Internet ad that may or may not have been seen by your target.

How do you make the right decision? To whom/what do you turn? Gut instinct does not cut it in many corporate boardrooms.

In Search of Support, Expertise, a Mentor, a Wizard...

When BOOM! began in the summer of 2003 it was a new experience for me. I had never started a company before. I had launched products, ideas, services, but never a company. My partners at the time, though available and supportive, were doing their own thing in other competencies in the company.

So I turned to other experts in the world who had built companies, turned around companies, and retained talent. From there I focused on who I wanted BOOM! to be.

Over the past decade, two books have formed the foundation of who we are and how we operate: *When Fish Fly* and *The Purple Cow.*

When Fish Fly speaks to how to create a vision and mission and rally the impassioned support of a team founded on commitment, accountability, and equal onus. *The Purple Cow* is all about being remarkable; truly standing out in the crowd, garnering attention and reviews, and, in so doing, you build a brand or a business.

In fairness to both books, my description is far too brief. If I were you I would grab a copy of each.

Why do I mention these books? At this juncture we are going to talk about making decisions. How do you make decisions, work with agencies, and try to build your businesses or brands? It likely comes as no surprise that I recommend marketers embrace risk taking. Operating outside of your comfort zone is the only key to growth – personally, professionally, and for your brand. There will be failures but there will also be huge successes.

At the end of the day all of you reading this book are also consumers. Quickly, think about the latest ad that you recall. Now if you are a client – would you have noticed your ad if you had not produced it yourself?

Simple question but I am hoping it is building some much needed personal awareness. Yes, some ads work – TV, radio, print – but most bounce off consumers like bullets off Superman. Truthfully, how often do you head into work the next day and think about them, let alone talk about them?

In his book, *The Purple Cow*, Seth Godin talks about Before, During and After Advertising. In the "Before" advertising world, word of mouth was the predominant media form. Someone told you about a product or service that served a need. Godin's "During" advertising period is also known as the golden age of advertising. Mass media, particularly television, allowed marketers to influence consumers directly. Companies placed ads and sales went up, almost magically.

Seth Godin also references some key learning from Sergio Zyman – well known as the guru who led most of Coca-Cola's rebirth in that golden age of advertising. Zyman was part of Coke's touchstone "Mean Joe Greene" and "I'd like to teach the world to sing" advertising that entertained and got attention. As powerful and memorable as those ads are for today's boomers, they translated into no incremental revenue. They did not see a measurable change in sales.

Godin characterizes the world of today as "After" advertising. It could be described as a post-advertising or digitally fragmented world. Mass advertising of the "During" advertising period rarely works anymore and word of mouth is glacially slow, chancy, and unpredictable. Thankfully, social media has put word of mouth on digital steroids. Ideas and conversations (unfortunately, mostly about celebrity news and gossip it seems) can diffuse at the speed of light, or whatever fraction of it data speeds across the Internet. It can also be harnessed, of course, to advertise products and services. Social networks like Twitter and Facebook can allow marketers to enlist consumers as advocates and also empower them to be their most powerful critics. That is not necessarily a bad thing as it keeps pulling marketers out of their ivory towers.

Awareness of all of the above hopefully leads you down the "yellow brick road" to the land of Adversperiential Marketing – where all good things grow!

Exhibit 3.3
Experiential Marketing Delivers Results

Event & Experiential Marketing Goals and Strategies

By far the top two overall goals and strategies for event and experiential marketing are to increase brand awareness and drive sales. Seventy-nine percent of brand survey respondents selected increase or create brand awareness as a key goal and strategy in the new survey up from 73% in the inaugural EventTrack survey last year. Increase sales was selected by 77% in the new study compared to 83% of brands in 2012. Rounding out the top five areas, according to brands this year, are to enhance product knowledge and understanding, gather leads, and influence deeper customer involvement.

	2012 %	2013 %	Impacted By	
			Advertising	Experiential
Increase / create brand awareness	73%	79%	✓	✓
Increase sales	83%	77%	✓	✓ + purchase on-site
Enhance product knowledge and understanding	53%	58%	1/2	★★★★★
Gather leads	48%	58%	✗	★★★★★
Influence deeper customer involvement	48%	52%	✓	★★★★★
Launch new products	48%	50%	✓	★★★★★
Build prospect database	45%	44%	drive to web	on-site & drive to web
Increase website traffic or Facebook 'Likes', social media activity	34%	36%	drive to web	on-site & drive to web
General media impressions / press coverage	38%	34%	maybe	✓
Conduct research, learn	23%	22%	drive to web	on-site & drive to web
Indentify, develop influential business-to-business brand ambassadors	17%	22%	✗	✓
Increae effectiveness of other media	16%	19%	maybe	✓
Identify, develop influential consumer-based brand ambassadors	22%	18%	maybe	★★★★★
Reduce price sensitivity	10%	8%	maybe	absolutely
Other	8%	4%		

Source: EMI/Mosaic EventTrack 2013
Note: The last two columns have been added by the author.

The Strategy of Experiential Marketing – Believe!

As you lay out your plan take confidence that the spend on Experiential – Adversperiential marketing is more than justified.

1. In 2012 investment in Experiential and Event Marketing grew to 5% (still very small) of marketing budgets in the U.S. This is up from 3.6% of typical marketing budgets in the prior year. (Event Track 2013 – Brand Report.) That's progress.

2. Objectives and strategies for briefs remained the same. When measured against any other tactic, Experiential Marketing can deliver the results as seen in the research in Exhibit 3.3 and the commentary on effectiveness that we have added beside it. Experiential Marketing works for consumers. We proved this in Chapter 2.

3. For brands using Experiential Marketing, it delivers on building awareness and increasing sales. For example, companies say they are 77% more strategically using Experiential Marketing to build their brands (see Exhibit 3.4).

4. Experiential Marketing delivers on objectives, works for consumers, and brands that have used it have proven it works for their business. Still nervous? While 22% of senior management is skeptical about Experiential Marketing's impact, they still believe that is it is necessary to their overall strategies. See what else CEOs think and how important Experiential Marketing is to their organizations in Exhibit 3.5.

Exhibit 3.4
Incorporating Experiential Marketing in a Strategic Plan

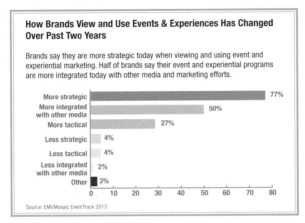

How Brands View and Use Events & Experiences Has Changed Over Past Two Years

Brands say they are more strategic today when viewing and using event and experiential marketing. Half of brands say their event and experiential programs are more integrated today with other media and marketing efforts.

- More strategic — 77%
- More integrated with other media — 50%
- More tactical — 27%
- Less strategic — 4%
- Less tactical — 4%
- Less integrated with other media — 2%
- Other — 3%

Source: EMI/Mosaic EventTrack 2013

Exhibit 3.5
What do CEOs Think about Experiential Marketing

How Senior Management Views Event & Experiential Marketing

Twenty-nine percent of brand marketing personnel say their senior management view events and experiences as critical and essential. This is up from 25% in the 2012 survey. Forty-three percent say events are considered an important part of the marketing mix to senior management.

- Critical, essential element of the marketing mix — 29%
- Important part of the marketing mix — 43%
- Necessary to strategy, but skeptical of the impact — 22%
- Not important — 3%
- Don't know / unsure — 2%

Source: EMI/Mosaic EventTrack 2013

Exhibit 3.6
The Marketing Mix

Importance of Event & Experiential Marketing to Organization

A total of 84% of the survey respondents say that event and experiential marketing is very important, critical or important to their organizations.

Very important, critical	38%
Important	46%
Somewhat important	14%
Not very important	2%

Source: EMI/Mosaic EventTrack 2013

Experiential Marketing works. Because it works better than many other tactics, and can be measured, it will continue to grow and make up a larger segment of the marketing spend. It will do this despite its "below the line" stigma among more traditional marketers. Why? Because consumers are engaged – events work!

If you take one thing away from this chapter, it should be to stop thinking of Experiential Marketing as a "below the line" tactic. It is your advertising brought to life. It is strategic and tactical. It is above the line and below the line – it is through the line! It is Adversperiential!

The bottom line? Do what is right for your brand. Put yourself in the place and time of your consumer. As a consumer you know what it takes to get your attention. Experiential/Adversperiential is more effective than any other strategy – from boardroom to consumer.

Still worried? Need more proof? Let me remind you of the new branded entertainment company created by Sid Lee and Cirque du Soleil.

Call it branded entertainment. Call it Experiential Marketing. Call it Advertising. No, call it what it is – Adversperiential Marketing! It is the destination at the end of the yellow brick road. Join me, and let's take the next step.

"The true sign of intelligence
is not knowledge but imagination."

Albert Einstein

"A question that sometimes drives me hazy:
am I or are the others crazy."

Albert Einstein

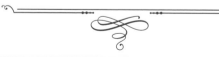

Chapter 4

The Journey to the Great Oz

BUILDING a PLAN that WORKS

"What shall we do?" asked Dorothy despairingly.

very day we ask ourselves, where to from here, what's next, "what shall we do?" A plan then unfolds based on a multitude of experiences and learning from our past, blended with considerations in the present and our perspective on the future. The challenge in today's cyclonic environment is the speed and lack of any sure footing. So many historical tried and true ways to build brands are ineffective and the future is spiraling at a ferocious rate. Knowing this and reminded of something that was shared with me many many years ago, "if traditions are so great, why not create some new ones," I headed into a learning and discovery phase that brings back my university days. With a cluttered hopeful head and a backpack with blank journals, my Mac and my phones, I headed to Cannes. The Cannes Lions Festival of Creativity is a marketing mecca – I was duly inspired and uncluttered!

The Marketers' Festival

Held annually on a little slice of heaven known as the French Riviera, for seven days every June Cannes attracts 12,000+ people from all over the world who are in the business of influence and engagement, specifically advertising professionals, designers, digital innovators, and marketers.

It's the biggest event of its kind for people in my business and seems to get a little larger and more successful each year. That success is not because of its locale, although the south of France is gorgeous, or the trophies, gorgeous too, by the way. It's who attends, or more precisely, who speaks.

My goal in attending was to gather global insights for this book and I most certainly did that. But it was also in the hopes of trying to make sense of the state of things – that is, where things are going, how to achieve success for brands, how to reach the ever-disrupted consumer. My conclusion? It's not going to be easy. There are many pathways to Oz.

Never have I been so riveted to my seat by an eclectic group of speakers, including designer Vivienne Westwood, rapper, actor, producer, entrepreneur, P. Diddy, journalist Anderson Cooper, and actor Jack Black. Famous names like these provide sizzle to the event. But where I learned the most as a marketer was from global leaders who manage global brands or agencies.

A Festival of Wizard-like Speakers

The Cannes roster of speakers included folks from Coca-Cola, Facebook, LinkedIn, Twitter, Saatchi and Saatchi, Disney – the list of heavyweights goes on and on and on. I tried to learn and listen to every single one and resist the urge to stroll the Mediterranean beachfront. Actually it was much easier than you would think because honestly the speakers were *amazing*! Whether you agreed or disagreed with their approaches and philosophies, for me it was marketing nirvana for eight to twelve hours a day for seven days. I'm a convert and I strongly recommend you make your way there at least once during your career.

The head of global marketing for Axe shared the evolution of the brand and what the company has learned along the way. It was truly amazing. Axe's brand promise to its teen male user is simple: "Axe gives guys the edge with girls." Over its 30-year history, Axe (or Lynx as it's known in the U.K.) has veered from sexism to a more feminist approach. What it has not lost is its sense of humor or its implicit promise that it will make those awkward teenage years a little less awkward.

Coca-Cola, one of the most influential and successful advertisers in the world, showed this year that it is also no slouch when it comes to Experiential Marketing. The soft drinks giant has deployed special live video-capture vending machines in both India and Pakistan in an effort to bring together citizens of those two oft-warring countries. Its award-winning effort encourages people to "Make a friend in India/Pakistan," and leveraging technology similar to Apple's Facetime, enables a live interaction with a person in the other city. The goose-bump raising effort likely does not fit your traditional definition of Experiential Marketing, but by connecting a soft drink with surprising and emotional meetings, it's a great example of Experiential, now known as Adversperiential, Marketing (a new spin on an old tradition).

Traditionally, advertising has been one-sided. A marketer uses a budget to build a megaphone – the bigger the budget the bigger the megaphone – and proceeds to shout at its target population. Today, however, most people don't want to be shouted at, and many take active measures to turn down the volume by avoiding advertising as much as possible. What they do want is conversations with brands that resonate with them. Thankfully, technology, such as social media, now allows us to do just that. Social media can create those communications between brand and consumer, it can also facilitate consumer-to-consumer communication about brands. That's why no marketing plan today can ignore social media.

The most important conversations are happening informally and not through paid media. They are happening at work, at our kitchen tables, at social functions, and over e-mail and social network circles. These conversations are authentic, organic, and can either kill or build brands.

If it was a perfect world (for marketers at least) and money and time were not an issue, we brand stewards would sit down with each and every potential consumer, have a conversation, and hopefully create that lifelong bond. Of course this is not feasible, budgets are limited, and priorities – and sacrifices – must be decided upon. That said, we need to do *something*!

Nathaniel Branden, a pioneer in self-esteem research and the author of numerous landmark works in the field, including *The Six Pillars of Self-Esteem* and *Self-Esteem at Work*, shared that "While all marketing attempts to speak to a perceived personal or business need, one of the most powerful ways we can connect with people is to make them feel understood not just on the surface, but deeply, and that is more readily accomplished face to face."

"Expanding the number of avenues – sensory, cognitive, emotional, etc. – with which an individual experiences the world heightens what they perceive and feel to be real. It's the difference between seeing the world in black and white versus color. The live experience provides a more intense sense of reality." I think Nathaniel is next to Oz in the Emerald City!

I am hopeful that you and your brand would like to join him. So, hold my hand, we are heading down the yellow brick road.

Rise to the Challenge – Be Not Afraid

The world is different and tomorrow it will be dramatically different again. You can play it safe and run with last year's marketing plan, with a few tweaks added, and hope it works better than the first one did. Good luck with that.

The world is no longer safe for marketers. Here's a distilled version of what I tell my clients:

> We are in a state of change so you need to be both wise enough to do what is sensible and courageous enough to take risks in order to build your business. If after you have written your plan your stomach hurts because you are pushing limits and going beyond your comfort zone, chances are that you are in a good place. And if you can sell it to others with conviction and passion, then you will win. You will bring your brand to life. This is

Adversperiential Marketing. This is what my team and I do for a living. Every day you need to show up, every day there is a new audience, every day you are selling yourself, every day there are those who applaud and those who critique – Adversperiential Marketing provides a stage for brands every day. Welcome to stage fright – every day. But welcome to the rewards too!

As I say all this tongue-in-cheek, I also say it with great respect for my clients and our industry and the discipline required to do great work. BOOM! has been successful because we are smart, disciplined, and crazy – a critical mixture of the three is needed to do great work. But it all starts with a plan that is stimulated daily by crazy!

There are *lots* of resources to turn to for building great brand plans. None really addresses the universe of Experiential Marketing. Shaz Smilansky explains the typical approach in his book, *Experiential Marketing*.

It is not uncommon for marketers to approach experiential agencies with briefs that describe in detail the above-the line campaign that they are about to run. This is because there is a tendency to ask the agency to implement experiential marketing activities that reinforce the above-the-line message and bring it to life. Often, they want to do this through a live brand experience that either replicates a TV advert creative or amplifies a similar theme that is a common thread throughout a planned campaign. (Shaz Smilansky, *Experiential Marketing: A Practical Guide to Interactive Brand Experiences* (2009), p. 29)

Well, we are here to help. Below is what we do with our clients in order to create great campaigns. It is actually a very simple four step – or brick – process.

- Brick One: Explore – See and Know
- Brick Two: Think – Brand Life
- Brick Three: Plan – Brand Path
- Brick Four: Do – Write the Brief

This is our cyclone safely dissipated that follows the yellow brick road to the Emerald City!

Brick One: Explore – See and Know

This is where you get familiar with your brand. Spend some time with it and explore the possibilities.

- **See:** So simple, just open your eyes and decide where you want to go. In our personal lives if we have a vision we say it, see it, and make it happen. Determine your vision for your business and your brand, then fiercely and relentlessly pursue that vision – every day.

- **Know:** Know your business. Know your marketplace. Know your competitive set. Know who you are, what you stand for, why you have some loyal followers and some naysayers – know, know, know. But know to the point of having an intelligent conversation. Do not get caught up in analytics that impede you from making decisions. Know what matters, focus on that and use that relentlessly to define your vision. My elevator pitch for "knowing" is, "Know what makes you famous and work it!"

Two examples illustrate my point.

Paula Green, a copywriter and former creative vice-president with DDB, spoke at Cannes. She helped create the famous "We Try Harder" campaign positioning for Avis, now 50 years old. That campaign has survived half a century because the company refused to do the fashionable thing and kill something that worked simply because it wasn't invented by the current VP of advertising.

"It survived because there was a vision: an underdog company that would turn itself inside out to improve itself, bolster its employees, and serve its customers," Green explained. "It survived because, despite management changes, agency changes, world changes, Avis stubbornly stuck to 'We Try Harder.' It was how they ran the business and their promise to their customers."

In honor of their 50-year milestone Avis ran the same campaign they had been running for 50 years. Thankfully no one in their organization has felt the need to change the vision and strategy. Sometimes I actually think it is that simple – define your vision, ensure it is relevant, stay focused, then live up to it every day. Evolve it over time but maintain its essence.

I once worked on Nestle Quik and you need to know my own children were Nestle Quik-aholics – they *loved* the stuff. And I loved the tagline from when I was a kid, "It's so rich and thick and choca-lick that you can't drink it slow, cause it's quick." I had been charged with relaunching the brand. We did some cool stuff and, as part of the proposal, I asked if we could bring back the jingle. Well you would have thought I killed someone. The room went silent and after the meeting I was asked to "think" before I made such radical suggestions. Are you kidding me – I was bang on! The return of retro goods and advertising all around us is justification. But, I was 28, so I shut up and sat down.

My point then and now is that brand equity is tough to achieve. So if you've got it, flaunt it. Today, I fall on my sword with clients and fight until they say, "*Enough!*" when I think something is right for their business. It doesn't always make me popular with the client (some love it and some hate it) but no one ever wonders if I care. I care!

Brick Two: Think – Brand Life

Become a Dr. of Thinkology. In the movie version, Oz awards a diploma to the Scarecrow in honor of his new brain. Truth is we need to think more; trouble is we need to do it fast!

Building brand plans against traditional thinking can no longer work because the world has changed so dramatically. A core idea like the Avis "We try harder" campaign can live forever but it needs to work within a plan that respects the current environment.

How do you build a plan today? How do you carve up your budgets? Should you still advertise and what happens if you don't? Isn't that the elephant in the room? The problem is that "traditional" is not working any more – it is time for some new traditions.

Fairfax Cone, founder of the Foote, Cone & Belding advertising agency, summarized the business succinctly when he said, "Advertising is what you do when you can't talk to someone." Which explains why we need to look beyond the traditional toolbox of media and seek other tactics to foster a dialogue that will build their brand, relationships, and sales. (Source: White Paper Creating Brand Connections TBAGlobal.)

How to think! Below is how we try to think at BOOM! It works for us. It helps us to ensure we are all aligned on the vision (the seeing) and the objectives (the knowing where we are and where we want to go). The thinking is the hardest but most stimulating part of all so lets begin.

Go for a walk, grab a coffee, head to a magazine shop or bookstore and a department store and grab materials, creative inspiration, take pictures, of lots of different things that you 'know' because of your understanding of your target that illustrate them, how they live,dress, what they eat, how they play, … you get it. Then move to Brick 2 on the yellow brick road and bring your brand to life!

Below is a structure that has served us well. Have some fun with your brand and bring it to life. Or call us, we love this stuff!

1. **Brand Boards:**

   Board A: Brand Visuals – Images of your product, the packaging, any advertising and where/how it is purchased. This all provides a context of what the world sees when it looks at your brand.

   Board B: Brand Target – Collage of what your target looks like – their clothes, what they eat, where and how they live, what they drive, their passions.

   Board C: Brand Vision – In five years what will your brand look like, where/how will the target buy it, use it.

2. **Build a Yellow Brick Road (*okay, that's a little self serving!*) Build a Map:** This path literally takes you from Board A to Board B to Board C. But, more importantly, it connects all three. There may be lots of arrows (see Exhibit 4.1), lots of things you need to do along your path – that is all okay.

Exhibit 4.1
Build the Map

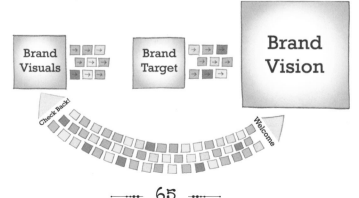

3. **Priorize:** Add some numbers – put everything in order of priority. At some point in this process you will have taken a break, grabbed a water or coffee, eaten an apple or cookie, and then headed back in. Taking a break is equally as important as building the plan. You need to step away and refresh before you can focus again.

Brick Three: Plan – Brand Path

This is your brand's life stages and story. Now you need to write it out, but keep the pictures and post them in appropriately. Here is a structure that may help you with the writing.

- **Vision:** State it. What is your vision. As an example our agency vision is to be "The First and Most Extraordinary Adversperiential Agency in the World."

- **Mission:** Understand your unique selling proposition (USP), understand what makes you famous and create a "manifesto" what will drive you to ensure it is relevant and competitive and motivating, to achieve, and to deliver the results you need. I love manifestos – they are powerful and motivating. For some inspiration in creating a manifesto and insights on just how powerful they can be grab a copy of *When Fish Fly*. There are two books that every person who joins our team is asked to read and this is one of them (*Purple Cow* by Seth Godin is the other one).

- **Target Consumer:** This is Brand Board B; it holds visuals of your target with words and research/facts that describe/define them.

○ Who are they – really?

○ How do they use your product?

○ Where do they buy it; why, and how often?

○ How loyal are they?

○ What does their life look like – where do they work, how do they dress, how and what do they eat, who is their circle of friends, how do they spend their leisure time, etc.

○ Their age matters but all of the above matters more.

○ And more, … if you have more that matters, add it.

- **Objectives:** This is Brand Board C, Vision – what you want your brand to be when it grows up.

- **Strategy:** This is the detailed roadmap (aka the yellow brick road) of how you are going to get from Board A to C, being respectful of Board B, and how they will evolve. Ideally you should author a three-to-five-year plan. The upcoming year is the most critical and in fairness is the one most in your control. You will need to check in on the upcoming years as you move along the path/yellow brick road. The point is you need a plan to get anywhere and should you alter the course, the vision and objectives will provide the guiding light.

- **Tactics**: These are the nitty gritty details – literally how much you will spend in each area, timing, etc.

- **Check In – Stay or Shift?:** Try to build in critical check points so that you don't get caught up in the cylone. These are times in the year when you check in, get a pulse on what is happening in the world, in the marketplace, and with your brand. Review, discuss, and keep going/stay the course or shift.

I love shift. With circles under my eyes, a coffee in one hand and an apple in the other, grey hairs reaching for the stars, I am drawn towards the cyclone. When people join our team as employees, supplier partners, or clients I promise them no 2 seconds, 2 minutes, 2 hours, 2 days, 2 weeks, 2 months, 2 years, will be the same. There will be no boredom. I love life, I love experiences, and this is why this book is in front of you.

Shit and shift happens – you cannot control it. With Adversperiential Marketing you are live with your consumer – the conversation is in full swing. When you are with a friend, you don't just halt the conversation, neither can you halt it with an Adversperience – hands have been shaken, eyes engaged, relationship in full development, and the onus is on you/the brand *not* to drop the ball!

Brick Four: Do – Write the Brief

Write the brief for your agency partners. Give them all of the above and more! This document will incorporate your knowledge of the brand, capture your Brand Boards, and put numbers alongside strategic and tactical plans.

I have attached a brief from a real live BOOM! client as a reference point (see Exhibit 4.2).

Exhibit 4.2
Real-Life Brand Plan for BOOM! Client

Fiscal Year :   **XXXX**
Company: **Xxx Xxxxx Xxx Xxx**
Brand Y: XXXX

Project Overview:

Bring to life Brand Y and ensure all initiatives are integrated

- **Establish Brand Y as a brand with "substance and style"** by engaging Brand Y's target consumers (Discriminating Men ~ 30-35) in a new, compelling and relevant way.
- **Drive the key message** of Brand Y as *"made with passion"*

The campaign will require the following deliverables:

- Campaign development illustrating the integration of Brand Y's positioning across all platforms:
  - Overall look and feel
  - Key message development
  - Key visuals
- Concept development and execution of any and all presented tactics
- Integrate the overall concept through the following support initiatives:
  - Elevated and retail-tainment program
  - Retail POS
  - Key Account event execution

Business and Marketing Objectives:

Brand Vision:
   Xxxxxxxxxxxxxxxxxxxxxxxxxxxxxxxxxxxxxxxxxxxxxxxxxxxxxxxxxxxxx

Business Objectives:
- Achieve XXXX sales of Brand Y nationally (+XX% growth)

Marketing Objectives:
- Build the perception of Brand Y as brand "current/on trend, sociable with substance"
- Bring to life the overall integrated engagement concept for all program initiatives and drive synergy across all support initiatives

Background:

- Brand Y is a focus brand for Company X, as the company is committed to win (grow share) in the Z category (key battleground); one way to achieve that is to gain momentum with Brand Y in XXXX segment

- Brand Y will receive "special funding" in FY'14 ....
- Every dollar should work towards brand building
- Bring to life the Brand Y idea and integrate it across all Company X's brand support elements
- The Brand Y internal working team conducted a workshop, developed the following vision and some corresponding ideas for consideration. Leverage the skeleton ideation and build upon it where applicable

Consumer:

- Who is our consumer?
  - He is financially secure and lives in a "cool" neighborhood
  - His handiness is driven by passion ie. He bought a house that needed a lot of work and methodically restored it into a beautiful bachelor pad. Now enjoying his home, he is in the process of restoring a sail boat.
  - He is entrepreneurial and a calculated risk taker
  - He is creative, and likes to explore
  - He likes fresh and local produce, likes going to the market and then making a good meal
  - He stays fit and enjoys his hobbies

- Where can we find and engage with this person?
  - Farmers' markets, artists' studios, unique furniture stores

- What kind of engagement will work?
  - Multi-sensory. Seeing craftsmen at work, seeing the tools, the process, the outcome
  - Learning, touching, being provided with a way to try
  - Being provided with ways to try, experiment and share on their own post engagement

- What is the big idea?
  - Brand Y's Big Idea is a program of education and exploration – an unexpected surprise that allows the target consumer to appreciate the quality and care that goes into this product. No mass production line here.

Requirements:

- **Big Idea Adversperiential Program**
  - Develop and execute an integrated campaign
  - Ensure call to action in all engagement
  - Investigate execution opportunities – is it possible to have adversperiences within multiple markets, online, offline,...
  - Develop the look and feel
  - Develop consumer experience
  - Work with brand to develop key messaging
  - Key asset requirements – brand guidelines
  - Devise a plan to maximize exposure given existing budget
  - How can the program be scalable?

Creative Assets:
- **Assets Available:** All visual assets from our Brand Y brand books, and other proprietary elements
- **Tone & Inspiration:** "XXXXXX"
- **Consumer Takeaway:**
  - BELIEVE: XXXX
  - FEEL: XXXX

Budget Guidelines:
- $1,750,000 (excluding fees)
  - **National Budget**
  - **Special Considerations**
    - **Regional Priorities**
    - **Key Accounts/Distribution Channels**

Now, do you see the importance, the potential? Do you feel the rush?!

This is your ten seconds of fame – make it worthwhile.

Every journey to the great Oz has its price – and this is yours – do the work. Follow the Yellow Brick Road:

Brick One: Explore – See and Know

Brick Two: Think – Brand Life

Brick Three: Plan – Brand Path

Brick Four: Do – Write the Brief

With your brief in hand enter Oz's circle of influence. This is where the magic begins!

We are always looking for the
perfect brief from the perfect client.

It almost never happens.

…

The response may not be great, but at least you'll
have the satisfaction of knowing you did the best you
possibly could, and you may learn something from it.

And you're always free to do an alternative
that does satisfy your creative standards.

Good briefs don't just come along.

…

Successful solutions are often made by
people rebelling against bad briefs.

…

Paul Arden

…

It's Not How Good You Are,

It's How Good You Want to Be

Chapter 5

Meeting the Wizard of Oz

CREATING an ADVERSPERIENTIAL CAMPAIGN

"We came here to see the Great Oz," said Dorothy.

The man was so surprised at this answer that he sat down to think it over.

"It has been many years since anyone asked me to see Oz," he said, shaking his head in perplexity. "He is powerful and terrible, and if you come on an idle or foolish errand to bother the wise reflections of the Great Wizard, he might be angry and destroy you all in an instant."

. . .

"You must keep your promises to us!" exclaimed Dorothy.

The Lion thought it might be as well to frighten the Wizard, so he gave a large, loud roar, which was so fierce and dreadful that Toto jumped away from him in alarm and tipped over the screen that stood in a corner. As it fell with a crash they looked that way, and the next moment all of them were filled with wonder. For they saw, standing in just the spot the screen had hidden, a little old man, with a bald head and a wrinkled face, who seemed to be as much surprised as they were. The Tin Woodman, raising his axe, rushed toward the little man and cried out, "Who are you?"

"I am Oz, the Great and Terrible," said the little man, in a trembling voice. "But don't strike me – please don't – and I'll do anything you want me to."

Brand Plan and Brief in hand, we skip out of our client's offices with notes scribbled over all of their decks and presentations. This is a "high" moment. Our adrenaline is rushing and the ideas are flowing. The key is to maintain this momentum and build a campaign. In fact, a few campaigns as the expectation is always that we will provide more than one, likely three, that will deliver the brand objectives and ensure an extraordinary Adversperience!

And this is where our wizardry begins. Actually it begins before we even walk in to take the brief. Then our hard work begins. Let me take you behind the curtain and share how we break it down!

The Process

1. **Pre-Brief:** A discussion is held with the key person on the account and the client to understand the scope and scale of the brief so that we ensure the right people are in the room when the brief is delivered. We always bring our creative team but there have been times when we bring our CFO. Sounds funny but its true! That said, we don't have a normal CFO, too. My point is that key people who will be helping to build our response to the brief, the Adversperiential Campaign, *must* be at the briefing. By the way, we don't charge for these bodies at the brief. In school you learn, "an ounce of prevention is worth a pound of cure." It is equally true when applied to building a campaign. If we have the right people in

the room at the beginning, the end product is better and we get to the end more effectively and efficiently.

2. **Brief:** Key client stakeholders need to be in the room. I am less concerned about who walks us through the brief. The key point here is that a brief stimulates dialogue. All the key brand stakeholders need to be in the room so that there is clarity and alignment.

3. **Next Steps and Check Ins:** Before leaving the room we all agree on what is next and when – sometimes it is 24 hours and sometimes it is two or more weeks. Regardless we stay connected internally as a team and with the client as there are twists and turns as we develop ideas so sometimes we will do a quick pulse check, without giving away the idea, to ensure we are not going too far off their yellow brick road! (*Yes, I know there are a few clients out there who are smirking. Okay, I will confess – there are times when we present a shocking idea. Sorry? No sorries actually!*) We don't present what we don't think will work. Sometimes we just have to push you to an uncomfortable place – this is usually the place where brands become leaders!

4. **We Think:** We talk, we brainstorm, we agonize, we walk, we run, we hit the gym, we have a drink at the bar (okay sometimes several), we grab a tazo chai latte and an apple, we draw, we grind our teeth and pull out our hair, and then somehow it all comes together. At some point we each have an "Aha moment" and great Adversperiential campaigns are born. And then we figure out how we are going to present it to our clients so that they see its magnificence and will let us do it. Because now, we are

in love and want to do it. We are now engaged, passionate and fiercely committed – so they must be too!

It's okay I am laughing at myself too at this point. It ain't that easy. Let me break down how we "think" and evaluate the merits of these thoughts in our effort to create extraordinary Adversperiences!

The Criteria for an Extraordinary Adversperience

At our agency we have a litmus test for every idea – it's actually pretty simple.

Turn a Head, Stir a Heart, Build a Brand, Make a Sale

- **Turn a Head:** Make the consumer want to engage, want to break stride, and want to check out what is going on. It sounds deceptively simple. It isn't, or my agency would have a lot more competition than we have today.

- **Stir a Heart**: Once the consumer is within the experience – keep in mind that the experience is happening at a time/place that "surprises and delights" the consumer and/or is a point of passion – it is critical that they are stimulated by the environment, what is happening, and that they want to check it out and engage.

- **Build the Brand:** While this is all happening, we start to build the brand, demonstrating through every sense implicitly and explicitly the brand's reason for being.

This is when and where it is important to communicate the brand's benefits and values and connect these to the consumer and their passions. Pull it all together so that the consumer gets it, so that they are relevantly connected to the product.

- **Make a Sale:** Yes, we can make a sale on site but that is not the point. If we have carried out the previous three components of our mantra properly, then the consumer will choose us/our brand when they have to make a purchase decision, be it next week, next month, or next year.

Assuming our campaign idea has passed the above litmus test, then the target will share this experience with others – in conversation, online and off, authentically and organically. This is the real payoff from a properly executed Adversperience. The conversation that is shared during the event and post the event, live or through social media networks is much more powerful (more meaningful, longer lasting) than any big budget TV commercial.

And, this experience or Adversperience is now forever ingrained in the consumer's mind because it is an "experience." It's indelible and they are forever touched and connected to the brand. A consumer/a human cannot unlearn, untaste, unhear, unlook, unmeet, or unexperience. We cannot undo that which we have experienced.

Traditional Advertising Versus an Extraordinary Adversperience

I have opened a pandora's box and the boxing gloves are being tied on. Before you raise your fists and prepare for heated battle/debate, let me explain.

Respectfully, traditional advertising historically has not concerned itself with the considerations that I will discuss below. Times, however, are changing as are agencies. Hence the reason that we are boldly taking the leap and naming ourselves as the World's First and Most Extraordinary Adversperiential Agency. We have been executing live experiences for years! Traditional "push, one-way" advertising is no longer effective. Advertising that is engaging and interactive is what works. To win, advertising must be a live experience. It makes perfect sense that an Experiential agency is the catalyst for this evolution/revolution. Embrace the evolution. Join the revolution!

I'm happy to engage in a healthy debate online at *adversperience.com* but til then, follow my line of thinking, my yellow brick road. The world is evolving, everything meaningful is Experiential, advertising is evolving to Adversperience!

As an Adversperiential agency, there are four considerations that we bake into every campaign.

1. *Everything Is Interactive*

Everything invites human interaction. Everything! The consumer looks, touches, hears, tastes. Every sense has the potential to be stimulated. It is a complete experience.

2. *Product Trial Is Authentic*

There is the opportunity for real product trial. Remember, nothing is ever real until it is experienced.

Until science fact catches up with science fiction and people can use their senses digitally via virtual reality, we are it. Face to face, person to person may seem old-fashioned in today's digitally distracted world, but it still works. So to everyone reading I would say let the consumer touch your product!

In no way am I diminishing a digital experience – they are real, valuable, and necessary but nothing replaces a live physical engagement.

3. *Resonance and Relevance Is the Magic*

I have used these two words more than any others in my career and will likely overuse them in this book. (*Sorry about that – but only a little.*) In marketing, resonance and relevance are truly all that matter. They are the measure by which an Adversperience *wins* over every other marketing initiative – hands down every time. And here is why.

- An Adversperience is two way and very, very personal so we can ensure that every consumer who enters the experience gets the information that they as individuals want and need – one to one, up close, and personal.

I mentioned earlier that if it was a perfect world you would have a personal meeting with everyone that is your target. That's close to impossible unless you are selling Lear jets and Bentleys. For the rest of us, creating an Adversperience gets you closer to that one-to-one ideal.

In the case of a car (of the mass market variety), the target may broadly be described as guys 30+, 60K+ income, entrepreneurial instincts, living in a condo, likely unmarried or in a relationship but no children yet.

An ad can certainly be created for this scenario. However, an Adversperience can speak to all the unique interests of everyone in the target group – the guy who wants performance and speed, the guy who like music and wants to know about the stereo, the guy who is a sports nut and needs to know where he is going to put his hockey bag, skis, golf bag, can the car tow a boat? You get my point. A 30-second ad that the consumer may or may not see cannot show and tell everything nor answer questions. An Adversperience can do it all and more. That's relevance!

- Do they get it, does it hit home, will they remember? And therein lies the magic of a good agency. How can we bring the brand to life in an unexpected way that ensures that the consumer remembers and then talks about? That is our ultimate goal for each and every Adversperience that my agency creates. Back to my earlier point that you cannot "un" try, do, taste something.

Here's an example that I think best illustrates resonance and relevance in action.

We were asked to build trial and awareness for a disposable razor targeted at 18-24-year-old males. We had no one else to lean on; there was no advertising or any other support for the brand. The benefits were simple: A 3-blade, high quality shave from a disposable razor that flexes and pivots. Now think about the 18-24-year-old guy. He does not want to stop and have this conversation about a disposal razor. End of story.

So we created a "mechanical razor" – think mechanical bull but custom built to be a razor. Consumers were given the opportunity to "ride the razor." Sounds goofy and/or painful but it worked.

- Year 1: It was the razor surrounded by mats.

- Year 2: It had a tent and scoreboard because we were now indoors, outdoors, on mountains, at beaches. The true validation came when we started to be asked to attend all sorts of events by organizers/promoters. "Asked" is the key word here because event organizers across the country were calling us and reducing or eliminating the venue fees that we would normally pay because they wanted the razor at their event. Here was a case of Experiential Marketing evolving into an Adversperience that was a win-win for truly everyone.

- Year 3: We added a DJ booth. The line-ups were insane. People sometimes waited four hours to "ride the razor."

We retired the razor but we still get calls today, people still talk about the program, and this razor continues to sell despite getting absolutely no advertising support. The fans who tried it and fell in love, remain.

This is relevance and resonance at their finest. We created an engagement that reflected the brand attributes in a way that connected to the consumer and to this day has maintained a base of loyal fans!

You sure can't ride a mechanical razor on TV, online, in a magazine, or on a billboard.

4. Ongoing Connection

This is where clients drive me crazy! This is where the ball, and usually the budget, gets dropped or put to the side. The connection with the consumer does not get maintained. We create an amazing Adversperience, connect to the target digitally for the purpose of maintaining loyalty and further amplification, and recommend that the brand maintain the conversation and appropriately stimulate purchase down the road. That is, stay in touch with your consumers.

None of the above is rocket science. To provide a framework, Exhibit 5.1 is what we call an Adversperience Campaign Concept map. We use it every day to build campaigns. It is a key tool to ensure we are developing integrated Adversperiential Campaigns.

Exhibit 5.1
BOOM! *Adversperiential Campaign Map*

BOOM! Adversperiential Campaign Map				
	Concept #1	Concept #2	Concept #3	Concept #4/Other Random Thoughts
Consumer Insight				
The Thinking				
The Idea				
How It Works				
Consumer Connectivity or Interactivity or Engagement				
Amplification Pre During Post				
WOM Expectations/Leverage				
PR Leverage				
ROI				
Rendering Topline				
Activation Timing				
Venues/Dist. Opp's				
Special Consideration				
Add Opp's				
Budget Context, Consideration Parameters				

I will close this chapter hopeful that my thinking is resonating with all of you and will reflect itself in your plans moving forward so that your brand can launch a balloon over the rainbow. Follow me along the yellow brick road to the launching zone!

Chapter 6

The Dangerous and Delightful Path to Oz!

PUSH the LIMITS!

*"You have plenty of courage, I am sure," answered Oz. "
All you need is confidence in yourself. There is no living
thing that is not afraid when it faces danger. The True courage
is in facing danger when you are afraid, and that
kind of courage you have in plenty."*

dversperience is *new* thinking and therefore revolutionary and therefore dangerous!

The intent of this chapter is to get very tactical and share with you how to bring an Adversperience to life, to manage your fear as you head into uncharted territory, and a bit of a danger zone. But before we get into it, let me share an example.

Anomaly is a great agency and one of the key brands they work on is Budweiser. I heard Franke Rodiguez from Anomaly present the "Red Light" campaign and I could feel his pain, passion, and ultimate reward!

The Bud brand team provided Anomaly with a brief. The essence of the brief was to "own hockey." (*Respectfully I am over simplifying but stay with me.*)

The Anomaly team toiled, brainstormed restlessly and relentlessly for six months going back and forth with the client with ads and ideas. Frustrated and at a loss after yet another meeting where everyone agreed they still had not nailed it, they headed to the bar. Several beers deep, one of the team suggested that they sell red lights – brilliant! For the non-hockey fans let me explain.

When a team scores a goal, when the puck is safely in the net, a red light above the net flares and a horn goes off. Hockey in Canada is a big deal and we typically gather with a few beers to watch the game. Anomaly's idea was to sell the Budweiser Red Light with a flare to Canadian hockey fans.

They created a fictious person, "Ron Kovacs," who, with his team, would come and install the light in your home and program it to go off whenever your favorite team scored. In addition to the light and the horn (with volume control) the unit can also be programmed to provide you with a warning that it is five minutes to game time so "Why not grab some Buds?"

The brand did not intend to make money from the lights. Their intent was to leverage the target's passion for hockey and intrinsically link it to their brand – brilliant.

This is a great example of an Adversperience. Multiple senses engaged, a multi-layered integrated campaign, magical results! You can only imagine the angst that the Anomaly team had when after six months they now wanted to tell the clients to sell Red Lights! This is definitely out of everyone's comfort zone but that is where leadership and victory lies.

So, let's dig into how we do this for your brand. While I have shared with all of you our concept map (Exhibit 5.1), this is a framework. It ensures we have dotted the "i"s and crossed the "t"s. The real fun begins when we actually have to create each detail of the consumer engagement.

The Adversperiential Continuum

Pre

We need to create some momentum. With the greatest of respect to all my clients, your target is not sitting at home waiting for your next product launch or campaign. We need to start igniting their interest, planting seeds, giving them a reason to engage.

During

At the point that they are engaged we need to tantalize every sense. Ensure the resonance, relevance and all the principles and parameters that have been shared in previous chapters are in place. Active engagement should be in full swing!

While actively engaging, we should also be collecting key information so that when the target leaves us they do so knowing the conversation has just begun.

Post and Beyond

As the target exits our physical grasp it is encumbent upon us to maintain the conversation. In maintaining the conversation we can strive to ensure they become and remain loyal users and more importantly ambassadors, sharing with their circles of influence relevant information about our brand. That action, by reference, further builds the size of the loyal group that then carries forward, ever amplifying. The return on investment (ROI) is priceless (but that is the subject for Chapter 7).

Exhibit 6.1 provides a visual representation of the pre, during, and post and beyond continuum of an Adversperience.

The Adversperiential Continuum

Given that an Adversperience is centered on human engagement, then it only makes sense that the continuum (typically a graph of sorts!) is human. And in place of the graph lines, I have used a human heart rate — the true measure of Adversperiential impact!

Pre **= Building the momentum**	**Ta Da! Showtime!** **= The Adversperience** **in full swing** Engaging, Sensory, Relevant, Memorable	**Beyond** **= Momentum is effectively and** **relevantly continued**
Consumer Heart Rate		
As momentum builds the interest of the target to break stride increases.	Now live, engaged and immersed in the Adversperience, the consumer's eyes are aglow their senses tingling their mind inspired and their heart racing!	With an inspired spirit, the consumer heads into their life forever connected and continuously reconnected through their own conversations and those relevantly stimulated by the brand. The intent, of course, is to maintain a strong and healthy heart rate.

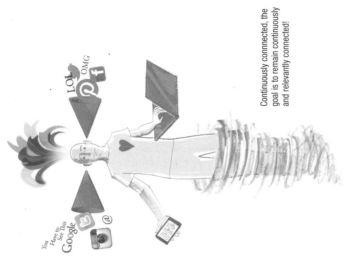

Exhibit 6.1
Pre, During, Post and Beyond

"Turn a head, Stir a Heart, Build a brand, Make a Sale!"

Magical Fairy Dust – Key Ingredients

The devil is in the details so without giving away all of our magic let me explain how we actually piece together an Adversperience.

I am truly fortunate, blessed, lucky, a blend of all of the above and more to have an amazing team. Together we have the wildest ideas and have proven we can make anything happen. We always solve for the marketing brief (see Chapter 4), but in cases where we think there is a bigger or a better yellow brick road, then we present that as well. These latter ideas are the ones that make clients truly think and the great ones take the risk and sell it with passion, as the results prove – witness the zany Ride the Razor program we shared in Chapter 5 or the Bud Red Light campaign shared in this chapter.

I know I am repeating myself a bit here as we travel along the yellow road from brief to map to now actually making it happen. Focused, inspired, and aligned we now click our heels and make dreams come true. Below are the key ingredients from which our fairy dust is made.

A Call to Action

A call to action engages the consumer. It causes them to think and makes them want to engage. We talked earlier about relevance and resonance – this is where it all comes into play.

Staging

Staging varies from uniforms or costumes to flashing lights online and off to massive systems that require days to install, like the Razor.

Collateral/Message Takeaway

The takeaway can be something tangible, like a relevant giveaway or a physical printed takeaway, that tells a little about the product, drives the consumer online with a purpose, and stimulates purchase (e.g., actual or virtual coupon).

Interactivity

This is the engagement piece. How will the brand connect with consumers? How will the consumer be greeted, what will happen when they enter the circle of influence? What will they see, hear, touch, smell, taste, think? And as they leave, have we closed the loop and ensured an ongoing relevant dialogue and ROI?

The Cast/Brand Ambassador

At our shop we refer to these folks as our "cast" because we legitimately "cast" them to a role. We match the brand target with the people who will be delivering the brand message. Casting is the most challenging part of every campaign we activate because of the very fact that we are dealing with humans who are dealing with humans and we are not in 100% control.

Brand ambassadors need to be highly trained, not just on the brand they are representing but on social niceties. They need to have amazing manners, great hygiene, and remember that whenever they are in uniform, they are on stage. They are brand mentors and role models and the world is watching – from consumers to clients to the press, online and off. Brand ambassadors are almighty, all powerful, and some days are the bane of my existence.

To them, activating a campaign is a "gig;" it's a shift. They fail to realize they carry the fate of months of work, planning, building, and a brand's resonance in a consumer's heart in the palm of their hands and in the words they speak. They fail to realize they are the last critical piece in a masterpiece and they hold the cards that determine the future fate of a brand and a client relationship.

In the past few years BOOM! has grown exponentially and as a result so has our "cast." At times our growth exceeded our focus on our historical micro-management of our Brand Ambassadors. Of recent, our micro-management has returned with a fury. We are powered by people and relationships so we are determined to ensure that only the most "remarkable" people work for us. Much easier said than done and a goal we strive for every day.

Time and Place

This is Adversperiential media. I think this is one of the most abused and/or misunderstood areas by people in my field. For me, while the staging and call to action is critical, equally important, if not more, is when and where we interact with the consumer. In fairness I have always hated "sampling," hated being interrupted as I am on my way somewhere – and I am always on my somewhere with great intensity. To that point, it has always been critical to us that if we are going to ask consumers to break stride, we had bloody well better make it worth their while. I will give an example that worked for me … well, sort of.

I was getting gas while my daughter ran in to get us Starbucks (the two places were connected). As I was filling up a young guy approached me in khakis and a blue shirt with the gas station's corporate logo on it. (*As an aside here and big call out to agencies – kakis and blue shirts are boring! I hate them and tell my people if I see them on any of our field teams that I will fire them.*) The young guy, clipboard in hand said, "I can save you money on your next fill-up and for all your fill-ups for the month – literally $0.05/litre and I can give you two cards if there is another driver in your family." I was interested but honestly, and he could read this on my face, I did not want to take the time. He could tell and offered, "We will have this done before your car is finished filling." So, I said okay. He asked a few questions, I signed, gave my e-mail, finished filling my tank, my daughter returned with our Starbucks, and off we went. As I left he did say I would be receiving the card within two weeks and the $0.05 offer would be good for the next month. Starting from when I received the card? Or from today? "Hmmm, not sure." Not a good answer. Okay a little bit of a let down here as really I was only going to benefit from the offer for two weeks

– if it was a one month offer and it was going to take me two weeks to get the card. That night I came home and mentioned to my cash-strapped son that gas credit cards would be coming and for a bit at least we would be saving a few cents and there were likely other offers as I knew that was how this chain operated. Well, as I type, it has been more than eight weeks and I still don't have my card!

Anyhow, back to my point. The time and place to interrupt my stride worked, the incentive/promotion promise was worthy but the delivery fell short and sadly it stays with me. I too am a consumer … aren't we all?

When we propose venues to clients for their brands we are very strategic in our thinking. We think through their volume expectations – the number of eye-to-eye interactions but balance this with where it makes the most sense from their target's perspective for them to engage.

With all due respect, rush hour at a bus or subway terminal is not always the most ideal time to engage. On the other hand, a women's consumer show may not always be the right place to showcase a women's product. Sure your target is present but so are a million other products so ensuring that consumers remember you as opposed to the others is even more critical. Whereas if you interacted with these same women at their office or in the salon where they get their hair or nails done you may have a home-run interaction.

In recommending where and when, we must carefully consider the elements of surprise, delight, and impact. Though I find the words surprise and delight trite, I use them often and buy into the thinking. I trust you have all been surprised and delighted in your life and know the feeling in your head and heart. This is what a brand needs to invoke in consumers. And, if done properly the impact will be both immediate and long term.

A good example of doing this is when we launched a men's razor product at car races. At the races thousands of men are onsite for several hours to several days. Between races they walk around and linger. Men tend to be very loyal to their razors, either based on performance or patterns (they have used it for years, why change). So, to alter their ways can prove to be challenging but at a car race where we can engage them and chat with them for a few minutes is ideal. They are open, willing, and able to chat, learn about the advantages of the product versus the competition. Our staging was very head turning, our staff costumed to match the staging, the engagement was fun, consumers all received a sample and some entered online onsite or when they got home for the chance to win prizes that connected the product to the event (upgraded seats, meet a driver, etc.), and the brand made efforts to maintain the conversation longer term – tough to do with men (they offered tickets to other races/performance events which connected the product to being better performing than the competition).

Maintaining the Connection

While the initial engagement and experience is critical, it is equally important to maintain a relevant engagement long after the event is over. Appropriate data capture not only delivers immediate ROI but can also ensure that the consumer stays loyal to the brand. This is something that traditional advertising cannot ensure. With an Adversperience we can keep talking with the consumer, asking them about changes we should make to product, finding out what other habits and passions they have so that we can further connect to them, and more strongly entrenching the product. And Adversperience is continuous. It is alive.

With all of the above, I trust you can now see the critical differences between advertising and Experiential Marketing (now new and improved to be Adversperiential Marketing).

Advertising hopes for 1, 2, 3, or more hits. It's a pushed message with hoped-for response by the consumer – immediate and long term once tried.

Experiential Marketing is a push-pull with eye-to-eye contact with the consumer.

Adversperiential Marketing dials both up a notch in that it has all the methodical strategic thinking that goes into advertising but executed live "with" the consumer, elevating the message to a live conversation at the right time and place (similar but better than a media plan) in the target's life.

And as opposed to advertising, with hoped-for and assumed results, an Adversperience can be measured, managed, and tracked to the moment. Please join me now as we follow the yellow brick road to the Emerald City.

Chapter 7

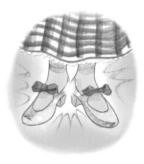

Riches in the Emerald City

DELIVERING RETURN on INVESTMENT (ROI)

"But then I should not have had my wonderful brains!" cried the Scarecrow.

"And I should not have had my lovely heart," said the Tin Woodman.

"And I should have lived a coward forever," declared the Lion.

"This is all true," said Dorothy, "and I am glad I was of use to these good friends. But now that each of them has had what he most desired, and each is happy in having a kingdom to rule besides, I think I should like to go back to Kansas."

nd they lived happily ever after. Ahh, the perfect ending to a once-upon-a-time tale that has its twists and turns of course, but always ends on a high note. This is always the anticipated/expected ending to a campaign. Did it pay off? Did it deliver? Did share improve? Was there top-line and bottom-line growth? Did we deliver a positive ROI?

Life, however, rarely follows a fairy tale script.

If only it were that easy – and yet for me, it is.

The ROI Formula

The simple truth is that ROI is very fact based. How we look at and structure the facts and assumptions is an art. Why an art? Because we have the potential to collect so much data and then need to weave it together into a story that provides actionable insights and measurable results.

The challenge is in determining what data/information to collect upon which to evaluate a campaign. This, of course, is a ongoing conversation. At some point in our careers, we've all said or heard that advertising and marketing is tough to measure. I would argue that we can figure it out.

We need to have some challenging but healthy debates and plot measurables as we begin to design the campaign. It is critical to begin with the end in mind

– identify the goals, objectives and any key learning and work backwards from there. I also want to make the case at this point that a live engagement, an Adversperience, is the ideal place and time to not only evaluate the short-term effectiveness of a campaign but to also collect critical brand information and engage longer term with the target.

Ideal for a few reasons. The real target, not someone from a list or someone with a fake identity, but the real person, present, vetted, and accounted for, is connected to your brand – they're right in front of you. This is the time to appropriately ask key questions and gain some critical insights. The icing on the cake is that you can ask some of these folks if they would like to continue the conversation, to be on a panel, to stay engaged and help build the brand – talk about building loyalty! Knowing that a brand is listening to what you think is very powerful, motivating, and bonding.

So, with this in mind, how do we calculate ROI, short term and long term? Follow the yellow brick road!

Research Wizards

I have two favorite research agencies that I work with and recommend when evaluating campaigns and ROI. Not surprisingly these companies are managed by two of my favorite people to chat with. The conversations are smart, energetic, peppered with hints of sarcasm, but always, always, always educational!

These two wizards and their agencies are Don Mayo from IMI and Corrine Sandler from Fresh Intelligence. (Their contact info is at the end of this chapter – feel free to use it.) They are not grounded in OZ but very authentically on planet Earth. I hope as you read you feel my no-nonsense passion and yet frustration for ROI. Let me explain.

To Don Mayo, I owe you a ton of money for all that you have done for my clients and my business over the years and for which you remain unpaid. To all you readers, no, I have never left an invoice from Don unpaid. But I have used his brain and his company's valuable data and resources countless times in an effort to help clients understand and calculate ROI. And on every occasion Don has risen to the challenge and almost every time the client has defaulted. They have said, "Yes, I want the information." Then when the budget is presented (always extremely reasonable; honestly from $10,000 to $50,000 to $100,000 depending on size and scope), they say, "No!" In fairness, the research budgets are always a small fraction of what is going to be spent on the campaign and yet I get a "No."

So, I ask all of you to help me, help you!

Embrace ROI

Let's not be afraid of ROI, let's embrace it! Let's agree to what and how it should be analyzed. Let's have the heated debates, let's argue, let's fight it out, but let's make it happen – or, honestly, get out! Okay, I will step out of the boxing ring now but I trust you get my point.

ROI needs to be measured. Below I will provide a "quick and dirty framework" for short-term measurement, but quality short- and long-term measurement needs an investment of time and money that I guarantee will pay huge rewards. The learning will not only ensure you are on the right track, achieving goals and objectives but, very importantly, building a loyal base of brand users and advocates that will represent your brand – your target becomes your brand ambassador – this is the pot of gold at the end of the rainbow!

I am sure many of you are familiar with the adage, "It's about the quality of time, not the quantity of time." Consumer engagement with traditional media is falling – I have shown this in previous chapters. I have also shown the rise in online media, however, the online world is the most cluttered, prolific, and fragmented medium. So does this offer the "quality" brands are seeking? It can if we execute an amazing live experience that captivates and engages the target in a space where they hear/know about it.

The challenge is making sufficient noise so that the consumer hears us. That said, many brands are quickly jumping online because the fear of finding other and better solutions challenges them so they "settle" with the *hope* of connecting to consumers through traditional and online means. They justify the concession by pennies, or fractions of pennies, per impression versus spending on one-to-one, eyeball-to-eyeball conversations. An Adversperience delivers quantity and quality because the consumer is engaged, typically for several multi-sensory minutes.

The Proof – The Research

Jack Morton,Worldwide, a noted U.S. agency, frequently publishes papers supporting our industry. In "White Paper No. 12 – It's About (Quality) Time: Experiential Marketing ROI," they address the topic of quality time.

- Difficult to define but increasingly important in the overall mix, experiential marketing comprises many tactics, including face-to-face (marketing through live interaction and events) and one-on-one (marketing through networked engagement, online and off). More important than tactical definitions is a bigger experiential strategy, based on the premise that today, audiences of all kinds (consumers, business partners, employees) want to be actively engaged by brands. They want brands to talk less, and do more. They are increasingly empowered to screen out messages they haven't asked for and may not believe – but under the right conditions they are willing to spend quality time interacting with brands.

- In one consumer survey, respondents said they'd spend an average of between five and 15 minutes interacting with a brand depending on the venue, and were willing to spend the most time with an experience in a retail or shopping mall setting.

Five minutes! Did you read that? Forget anything more than that, just focus on the five minutes. So, why do marketers continue to spend significant dollars developing (agency fees, creative development), creating (talent, venues, staging), producing (editors, writers, production teams), and airing (TV, outdoor, print, radio, online, offline) with the *hope* of gaining 30 seconds of attention that so very easily can be distracted?

Interestingly, B2B marketers get it. Where do they spend most of their time? They talk to their key constituents one to one, in meetings or at trade shows.

In addition, Experiential Marketing moves people through the purchase funnel very quickly (see Chapter 2). In relatively short order, sometimes in a single interaction, participants are moved from awareness to purchase. The potential result is higher rates of sales conversion in less time, and therefore better ROI. Compare that result to the typical "rule of seven" for traditional advertising, which posits that it takes seven ad exposures to deliver a sale. (Source: Jack Morton, Worldwide, "White Paper No. 12 – It's About (Quality) Time: Experiential Marketing ROI")

Add to this the impact of consumers sharing their experience with others and the impact is exponential. "According to a recent Event Marketing Institute study, 90% of those who told friends and family about participating in a brand experience (78% of those surveyed) did so within just two days." (Source: Jack Morton, Worldwide, "The

Viral Impact of Events. A Study on the Power of Word of Mouth Strategies to Increase the Impact of Your Events")

Let me recap:

- Consumers will spend 5-15 minutes with a brand at an event or venue.

- Experiential Marketing moves people from awareness to purchase quickly, with higher rates of conversion and loyalty than traditional advertising.

- Ninety percent of those who attend an event tell others within two days.

Help me to understand why you would not invest in Experiential Marketing. If you are still not a believer – Ugh! Keep reading. Call or e-mail me.

For the believers and those who are going to embrace Experiential Marketing and dial it up a notch and commit to Adversperiential – read on!

The Seven "I"s of ROI

When we present our company credentials we outline ROI. It is a key slide. I am a strategic marketer at my core so the letters ROI are critical to me. However, I am also a key creative lead at our agency and believe there is so much more to ROI and I play on the real value of "I." My thinking is backed up by a comment made by Albert Einstein (also noted in the Jack Morton's White Paper No.

12), "Not everything that can be counted counts, and not everything that counts can be counted."

Here are my seven "I"s for ROI.

Investment

This is standard, of course.

Did the campaign we created and executed pay back? Were the dollars spent justified?

These questions are answered using a simple calculation, assuming we agree on how it is calculated, of course.

> Total dollars divided by # of interactions
> (or product samples or impressions)

In fairness, I usually recommend that we ensure we correctly account for the total dollars spent. For example, if you are going to use a piece of staging for multiple years, allocating the full cost to the ROI in year one will mean a low Year 1 ROI and likely a very high Year 2 ROI.

Exhibit 7.1 provides an example. I have tried to keep it simple because ROI is something that you can easily complicate.

Exhibit 7.1
Calculating the Investment

Example 1: A Typical Simple ROI Calculation	
Total Budget	$650,000
Any materials or staging that are used for more than 1 year should be divided by the number of years they are used (e.g., vehicles, staging, etc.)	
= 250,000 with plan for 2 years use (125,000/year)	- $125,000
Dollars spent in current year on campaign	
= 650,000 – 125,000 =	$525,000
# of Samples Distributed Does not include sample cost of goods	500,000
Cost per sample: = $525,000/500,000 =	**$1.05**
# of Impressions	14,000,000
Considers number of events and venues visited and a realistic number of people who would have seen campaign	
PLUS	
We evaluate the media impressions from:	
• tour route if a vehicle is used	
• social	
Cost per impression: = $525,000/14,000,000	**$0.037**

This quick and dirty calculation only provides a starting point. It measures the short-term cost without identifying the short- or long-term value, which is the greater benefit when you execute an Adversperiential campaign. Nor does it speak to quality of time, the true awareness, share of heart, spirit, and all of the "I's" noted below that are the magic of an Adversperience versus all other strategies.

Imagination and Inspiration

How do you evaluate return on imagination and inspiration? During events, we ask people "why" they came over to our venue and we record their answers in writing, with a picture, with a video – we capture verbatims.

But for me, capturing imagination starts in our brainstorming sessions, translates into our presentations, and then manifests itself with the end target. If we have triggered a spark in ourselves and then done the same when we present to our client, it is very likely that we will inspire the target.

When we have a great "Call to Action" or staging that makes a consumer break stride, I often wonder what part of the target's mind and/or imagination we have triggered – inspiration and imagination are very personal. Where did their mind wander and why did they break stride?

While we capture verbatim responses, our very best feedback has come from our brand ambassadors. These are the field staff who meet, greet, and engage consumers at all of our activations. Our field staff often tell us that they like to work on BOOM! programs versus programs for other agencies because they are fun and different. The ambassadors go on to explain that they are excited by our programs, they are different, stand out, there is engagement on many levels. Perfect – check mark!

Innovation and Ingenuity

"Cool" is still relevant. "Cool" is timeless. And "Cool" is often what consumers share. "I saw the coolest thing today."

The trick is finding cool, ensuring it is relevant to what you are activating, and then incorporating it so that it is interconnected with the product/product message so that an indelible link is made or leveraged.

Cool has a halo effect.

Intensity

For me, there needs to be a degree of education that permeates through the engagement. With Adversperience the medium is the message. It is critical that messaging be intrinsic in every element from flooring to uniforms to the words brand ambassadors share.

- The short-term effect is that the consumer makes an immediate connection – "they get it."

- The long-term effect it that they become loyal, that we have reached them on a deeper level.

Insight

We have always had the ability to gain insights from consumers, though often they are in the form of unstructured verbatim feedback. This is not to say we do not apply structure or guidelines, we do. But, we often do not have the budget "luxury" to use an external research agency. I have never really understood why research is a luxury. Good research is priceless and since we are having one-to-one conversations with consumers every day, why not ask them a few good questions.

Impact

This is the bottom line. Did we have an impact? Did we drive trial, awareness, brand equity, purchase, repeat, word of mouth?

All things can be measured and monitored but you need to spend some research dollars. My advice is spend the dollars. It's nice to track share and see how you are doing but, what does that really tell you. If sales and profits are growing (which means you are not price cutting, typically), then you are likely driving share. Isn't it more important to understand what it takes to get more and more consumers to try your product and fall in love with it and so on and so on and so on?

"I"

The only thing that really matters – from brand owner to consumer!

At the end of the day, if what is being done to build your brand doesn't rock your world, make you proud, make you want to tell your mom, it is not going to rock anyone else's!

Hopefully I have done Einstein proud! A healthy balance of measureables and unmeasurables.

In the Real World

Truth is it's tough to sell an unmeasurable in a boardroom. The ROI question still prompts migraines for executives at some of the best consumer packaged goods companies on the planet. Procter & Gamble, America's biggest advertiser, said in 2013 that it was starting a major review of its $5-billion-plus annual marketing budget. This, just two years after launching a new system to measure its ROI, or ROMI (Return on Marketing Investment). P&G wants to do a better job measuring digital media (such as social and search) and find out what is behind sales trends that traditional models can't. (Source: "P&G Launches Major ROI Review," Ad Age, May 20, 2013 at *http://adage.com/article/news/ procter-gamble-launches-major-roi-review/241565/*)

When advertising's biggest spender says it is not sure about its ROI, marketing and advertising professionals should shudder. If you can't prove what you do works, you are in deep trouble. Don't worry I am not going to leave you with rhetoric.

Below follows how to go about tracking and evaluating Adversperiential ROI. A special thanks goes to Corrine

Sandler of Fresh Intelligence. The framework below comes from a presentation she made with me to a client. It is abbreviated because this book is about Adversperiential Marketing, not research. If you want to know more, call Corrine or read her book, *Wake Up or Die: Business Battles Are Won with Foresight, You Either Have It or You Don't.*

1. **Define Your Objectives:**

   - **Sell Products:**
     - Gross sales per time period, before and after the event.
     - Change in length of sales cycle.
     - Change in intent to purchase.
     - Change in traffic to website or brick and mortar locations.

   - **Launch New Products:**
     - Increase in market share
     - Increase in market penetration.
     - Number of qualified leads for new product lines.
     - Ratio of new to existing customers.
     - Ratio of new to repeat visitors to website.
     - Increase in depth or breadth of customer base.

   - **Drive Affinity between Customers and the Brand:**
     - Increase in brand engagement.
     - Increase in awareness.

○ Increase in preference.

○ Increase in exposure and spread of company name, brand, products.

○ Increase in company or product knowledge among targets.

- **Reach New Markets and Customers:**

  ○ Increase in new market-specific sales leads.

  ○ Increase in awareness or preference or intent to purchase.

  ○ Increase in mindshare.

2. **Determine Your Measurable Criteria of Success**

- If awareness is your ultimate goal, success may be determined by the increase in unaided awareness of brand/product.

- If your objective is to move (sell) product, success might be measured by incremental sales or traffic increases after a program/event took place.

- The potential metrics used to measure success:

  ○ Percent of attendees more likely to buy.

  ○ Percent of attendees remembering the brand.

  ○ Number of qualified sales leads generated.

- Conversion rate of attendees.

- Total potential sales (no. of attendees x conversion rate x average sales).

- Total exposure of key messages in resulting press.

- Social media.

- Percent conversion from a specific event website to a corporate site.

3. **Set Benchmarks**

   - The key point to remember about any evaluation progrom is that measurement is a comparative tool. You need to compare one set of results to something else. Review past event metrics as well.

4. **Design a Measurement Plan**

   - This plan has to be tested and proven to be an effective measure of your defined objectives.

5. **Define Your Specific Metrics**

   - Percent change in perceptions.

   - Percent change in awareness.

   - Percent increase in preference.

   - Percent of attendees likely to purchase.

   - Cost per lead.

   - Cost per qualified lead.

   - Cost per customer acquisition.

   - Cost per minute spent with prospect.

   - Visibility and prominence.

As we close this chapter I hope you feel as though if you embrace and activate an Adversperience, your wishes can be granted and "happily ever after" is achievable. It means some solid strategic thinking up front, relevant analytics, and wise gut instincts. It's a healthy balance of the three. And, I would ask you to please spend the money and do the research. As I said earlier I guarantee it will be worth it.

As promised, here is the contact information for Don Mayo and Corrine Sandler.

Don Mayo
Managing Partner, Global
IMI International
USA*Canada*UK*Australia
T 416.440.0310 x231
C 416.505.7545
F 416.440.1768
dmayo@consultimi.com
www.consultimi.com

Corrine Sandler
CEO
Fresh Intelligence Research Corp.
T 416.342.8225
C 416.450.8151
www.freshintelligence.com
csandler@freshintelligence.com

Chapter 8

A Brain or A Heart?

CONNECTING with CAUSES and SPONSORSHIPS

"I shall take the heart," returned the Tin Woodman; "for brains do not make one happy, and happiness is the best thing in the world."

ow I love thee? Let me count the ways." Isn't this how we all speak to all the brands we are marketing?

When consumers get up in the morning and turn on the coffee maker, we are responsible for marketing the "savor the cup of coffee" campaign we executed six months ago. Is this not their response? Yes, I am being sarcastic, but sarcasm is not my intent; humor, humility and a much needed dose of reality is.

I always find it comical when a client says this is the "biggest launch" or "On October 1 we are launching XXX and it will change everything and by the way my target is a lifestyle conscious, van-driving soccer mom with 2.5 kids" or "a 25-year-old fresh-out-of-school, in-their-first-career, dresses-like-a-hipster, shares-life-on-facebook male," … any of you want to jump in here? Do not deny that you have either said or heard these words.

Whether it is the mom or the 25-year–old, I think I can, with great confidence, say the general public is not waking up in the morning and pontificating your brand. Sorry about that. They are, however, waking up in the morning and trying to navigate life and that is where brands come in. Hopefully I have already made this point.

Turning a Head

Brands can intertwine very relevantly and remarkably with consumers. They can etch a place in their heart and soul and make navigating through life nicer, easier, and, from that perspective, a person may – and I would argue *will* in fact – fall in love with a brand.

In previous chapters we shared our mantra for activating Adversperiential campaigns: "Turn a head, stir a heart, build the brand, make a sale." The intent, of course, is to get consumers to look, be intrigued, and choose to break stride. Then once they are engaged, pull at their heart strings with the brand story and in so doing build the brand and their loyalty to it and encourage them to purchase the brand. But, there needs to be more.

Just as people evaluate their life, their noble purpose, so too should brands. "Human beings are powered by emotion, not by reason." (Source: Brian Sheehan, *Loveworks: How the World's Top Marketers Make Emotional Connections to Win in the Marketplace* (PowerHouse books, 2013), p. 16) And therein lies the magic of connecting a brand to a cause or sponsorship. It connects to the consumer on an emotional level, turning the head and stirring the heart of the overly busy soccer mom and the 25-year-old!

The Story

Causes, sponsorships, and endorsements are used to further activate human emotions. In all cases there is an incremental story – that of the cause or sponsorship property or endorser – and, as such, the brand benefits from the halo credential, otherwise known as an "image transfer." This is the goal.

And as I am working on this chapter I receive an e-mail that a refreshed "Causes" website has been launched that provides people with "stickers" they can put on their various social media networks that identifies what they support. Other functions will allow them to see which brands leaders and celebrities are supporting. See and be seen having an impact on the greater good.

Before we debate value let's clarify these marketing events.

Cause Versus Sponsorship Versus Endorsements

Each of these niches have their own shelf in bookstores and their own associations, so for the purpose of this book I apologize for keeping things clean and simple.

Cause Marketing:

- When a non-profit and a for-profit corporation partner together with the purpose of advancing the mission-related work of the non-profit, and the marketing goals of the corporation. (Source: *The Non-Profit Times*, October 1, 2013)

Sponsor and Sponsorship Marketing:

- To *sponsor* something is to support an event, activity, person, or organization by providing money or other resources in exchange for something, usually advertising or publicity, and always access to an audience.

- *Sponsorship Marketing* is the activation or leveraging of this sponsorship, beyond the usual advertising, publicity, and audience access.

- *Sponsored Properties* can include venues, events, personalities, organizations, entertainment programs, or media properties. (Source: The Sponsorship marketing Council of Canada at *http://www.sponsorshipmarketing.ca/sma/categories.asp*)

Endorsements:

- An act of "giving one's public approval or support to someone or something" (Source: Dictionary.com)

- A recommendation of a product.

The point I want to make is use these methods to better and more relevantly connect with your consumer. Show and tell your consumer what you stand for by virtue of what you connect with/support. The same thing can be said of your own circle of friends – guilt by association. Your circle says a lot about you. It is also why brands disassociate from celebrities when they make choices out of sync with brand values. Again, guilt by association so choose, but choose wisely.

Being Effective

I have attended a myriad of leadership and marketing conferences, seminars, and expos. A study by neurologist

Donald Calne continues to be mentioned. His critical finding: "The essential difference between emotion and reason is that emotion leads to action while reason leads to conclusions." In other words, there's a real payoff when you strike an emotional chord with your target group.

Annette Simmons, an expert in storytelling further explains, "When you tell a story that touches me, you give me the gift of human attention – the kind that connects me to you, that touches my heart and makes me feel more alive." (Source: *Loveworks*, p. 16).

Typically cause and sponsorship marketing provide a framework for engaging live with people. They are typically events and therefore make an ideal place to activate an Adversperience. Build the Adversperience as noted in previous chapters then integrate it into the cause event or sponsorship in a way that is meaningful or relevant and the consumer will remember you.

But do it right and think it through as the level of consumer/stakeholder emotion at these events is higher than when you interact with them while they are shopping or at work, for example. In a cause situation you are dealing with matters of health, poverty, socio-economic conditions – intense topics – so if you choose to connect your brand then do so respectfully. Sponsorships, though they have the potential to be equally as intense, tend to be more about interests – cars, sports, etc. They deal more with life's niceties than its challenges. Celebrity endorsement for me is very esoteric. I am biased as

I would rather see a real person I can relate to using a brand than a celebrity, but I know I am often out voted here. My comment is be careful. Celebrities have human frailties that can quickly cause unforeseen challenges and your brand may be an innocent victim.

Considerations Before Undertaking

All of the above said, my team and I have used all three very effectively over the years. Before I share some case studies, I would suggest you consider the following points before you engage.

- Do you have the money to support your brand and the initiative with which you are partnering? A logo on an ad or on a ticket, a program, a rink board, or a jersey stakes some very visible real estate and impressions but that is not enough. In the spirit of truly engaging the stakeholder you seek, explain why you are connecting to the partner, tell the story, bring them into the conversation, and then explain how this connects them and your product. Wrap it up into a neat and tidy package. Don't assume people will get it. Tell them what there is to get! Bottom line: a sponsorship message is typically a more complicated story to get across to consumers. It might prove to be more powerful over time than a more straightforward commercial come-on, but you have to be prepared to put the time, effort, and, yes, money, into it. "Sponsorship without activation is like an electric toy without batteries." Author Unknown

- Be opportunistic, but know your place and time and show respect. There is a place and time for everything. Just like celebrities, trends come and go, so you need to be aware of what is relevant for your consumer. And you need to ensure you are aware of the emotional connection consumers have to causes so connect to the cause with grace. I remember when recycling was a competitive advantage, now it is the cost of doing business. What is the hot button or unvoiced competitive advantage that can be turned from a curiosity to a market share winner?

The point is that the premise of cause or sponsorship marketing is that it augments what your brand stands for. It partners your brand with like-minded consumers. And the impact of this is that it further develops your brand story and, given the heightened emotional connection implicit in a cause, sponsorship, or endorsement situation, the impression is indelible and the value is priceless. An Adversperience connected to any of these properly has an exponential impact. Remember that when evaluating ROI, the loyalty meter for your brand likely rose tenfold!

Marketing2020 conducted some research this past year among the world's leading marketers. They asked them to "Agree or Disagree" with a series of statements.

- 73% agreed with the statement "I believe that brands with a clear societal purpose will drive more business growth." 6% disagreed.

- 84% were proud of the brand's societal purpose.

- 60% claimed to ensure that employees were fully engaged in the purpose.

- 63% said they continuously engage consumers and customers around the brand's purpose.

A Little Love and Support Always Works

I think intuitively we all understand and agree that we attend events or connect to causes because they strike a very personal chord within us. Therefore it only makes sense that when brands leverage these opportunities they are trying to reach and connect to that chord.

There are prolific examples of both. In the case of sponsorships we can start with the Olympics and go from there. Virtually every sport, every sports facility, and every key athlete are in some way sponsored by one or many different brands. While sports is one example there are equivalent examples for every passion from music to art to dance – the list is endless.

A prolific list of examples also exists for causes. But for me the proverbial "chord" with causes is stronger, more intimate, and therefore more tender. Causes cut to our very core. Below is an incredible and heart wrenching example.

The Bridge of Life. The interactive bridge that speaks to suicides. From Samsung Life Insurance.

This campaign was presented at Cannes. It deservedly has received a ton of awards but more importantly, it has saved lives.

Below the details from the *samsingvillage.com* website.

Bridge of Life Reminds You of the Good in Life
June 25 2013 at 8:41 AM

Among some 30 bridges that span across the Han River, which runs through Seoul, is a special bridge that talks to you when you need someone to keep you company.

- *"Are you not tired?"*

- *"Is there something on your mind?"*

- *"Why don't we forget everything and go watch a movie?"*

The kind words are lit up on the guardrails of the Mapo Bridge as you walk by. The soothing and comforting words are meant to change the minds of those who come to the bridge to take their own lives.

Of more than 1,000 cases where a person jumped off a bridge over the Han River during nine years between 2003 and 2011, most of them – about 17 percent, to be more precise – took place at Mapo Bridge. In efforts to prevent such cases, Seoul City and our Samsung affiliates – Samsung Life Insurance and Cheil Worldwide – teamed up for a "Bridge of Life" campaign.

The project sought to create an interactive bridge that communicates with the people so that they can change their minds about suicides. Motion sensors were installed on the guardrails so that messages light up in line with the footsteps of the passers-by.

These are messages of love and care – words your families and friends would share with you during times of hardship.

In the middle of the bridge, there is an Image Zone where photos of happy children, laughing school kids and smiling grandparents are displayed to remind people of the precious moments in life. There is also a brass statue of two friends sitting on a bench – one consoling the other – named "One More Time" – to motivate people to give another go at life.

The campaign received the Grand award at the 2013 CLIO Awards, as well as a Gold in the Public Relations category and a Silver in the Engagement category.

But more important than the recognition it received at the world-renowned awards ceremony is that the campaign helped redefine Mapo Bridge as a place of healing for those who encounter troubles in life.

No matter what kind of hardships we sometimes get into, life is good. And we all need to be reminded of that from time to time – like the messages on Mapo Bridge, the Bridge of Life.

For those of you who would like to see how the Bridge of Life helps provide a new motivation for life, please take a look at the video link below.

www.samsungvillage.com/blog/2013/06/bridge-of-life-reminds-you-of-the-good-of-life.html

Hope you agree the above example is heart wrenching and touching at the same time. Please grab copies of *Lovemarks* and *Loveworks* – both are filled with examples of brands leveraging causes and sponsorships in an effort to better connect to consumers and in so doing also make the world a better place.

The truth is as humans we crave happy endings, anything that tugs at our heart. Hollywood figured that out long ago. The hero always – well, okay, almost always – gets the girl and they drive off into the sunset. Turn your brand into a hero and your consumer will fall in love forever. This is the yellow brick road to real "riches" in The Emerald City.

Chapter 9

Unexpected Paths and Pleasures

SAMPLING and RETAIL-TAINMENT

"But I don't understand," said Dorothy, in bewilderment, "How was it that you appeared to me as a great Head?"

"That was one of my tricks," answered Oz. "Step this way, please, and I will tell you all about it."

orothy and her friends certainly encountered a series of surprising and unfortunate, events while on what they thought was a direct route to The Emerald City. And that relates to the whole point of an Adverperience – to get people to graciously/pleasingly divert from their plan, engage them, win them over, and convert them into brand fans.

Consumers are on a mission and sampling/retail-tainment diverts them from their plan, at store level. That is, of course, why sampling and Experiential Marketing were created in the first place – to get a consumer to try something new or switch brands. Adversperience is all about drama and experience implicit in "surprise and delight!"

In earlier chapters we talked about consumer discontent with the retail experience – it's boring. To spice things up a notch, fashion retailers are bringing in DJs to spin, others have special event nights, parties. The goal is to make the retail experience more fun.

The Original Sampling Experience

I'm not sure who invented sampling or retail-tainment. Sometimes I feel like a baker or cheese maker in a small village routinely trying new recipes, where the true test of the product's marketability was to have patrons (who they all knew by name) try it when they came into the store to get their goods. Consumers either "tried and buyed" or the proprietor went back to the drawing board. Seems so authentic and simple, doesn't it?

Today, sampling and/or retail-tainment is a sales and distribution strategy first, a marketing strategy second. When brands are launched or promoted and sampling/retail-tainment is used as a tactic, it is usually accompanied by a flyer ad, in-store feature price, or significant volume order. The sales rep who negotiated the retail order was putting together a package deal based on hitting some volume targets. Nothing wrong with these objectives, except that the value and therefore the quality of the sampling gets diminished.

Walk into any Costco around lunchtime and there is actually no need to buy lunch. You can sample your way through your shopping experience. Or for some dedicated "Costco Grazers," the goal is to sample until full and leave. It is not the vision that Costco's marketers had in mind when they were putting their "in-store sampling" program in place, but clearly the ranks of grazers is not small enough to be ignored. Costco's program is sampling at its stomach-stuffing best, but it leaves a lot to be desired entertainment-wise. Sampling works. It gets much needed trial and drives purchase, but to achieve long-term brand loyalty it must go further than a "gut-fill" experience.

Retail-tainment Is Not New, It's Named … Kinda like Adversperience!

Rightly or wrongly, I want to attribute the term "Retail-tainment" to Walmart. I feel like they coined this term (and or started using it aggressively) when they launched an in-store sampling program for all their suppliers/vendors. Their intent was to dial sampling up a notch. Walmart took the concept and ran with it.

Take for example, a 2010 retail-tainment effort to promote the DreamWorks Animation film, *How to Train Your Dragon*. Walmart's effort consisted of more than 2500 replica Viking ships in a special section of its U.S. stores that also happened to feature more than 100 movie-themed items for purchase. Over the years, Walmart has also lured in big boys with Nascar-themed retail-tainment events and women with tie-ins to female-focused magazines and cosmetics manufacturers.

Walmart learned long ago that an entertained and emotionally engaged shopper is a heck of a lot better than the alternative. And kudos to them.

But, not all brands have made the investment noted in the examples above. In fact most have a demo cart with some signage and a brand ambassador in a uniform. That's Sampling 101.

Sampling and Retail-tainment Outside the Box

Call it sampling or call it retail-tainment, today the two are executed very similarly by most marketers. Few brands have the budgets to create *huge* in-store events. While the intent may be the same, many executions fall short. Take a simple pop-up table or cart, some signage, a not-so-engaged person in a uniform, and little pieces of cut up product for people to taste, touch, smell. Welcome to my nightmare! While this certainly does create trial and moves product, is there not a better way? There is and we have done it, but it means thinking and executing outside of the box and that is a challenge for brands and retailers.

For a brand that cleans clothes we came up with the idea of a clothes line and a faux washer/dryer that rolled. Our brand ambassadors were in "scrubs." The intent was to use the washer/dryer surface as the demo table.

The brand team loved the idea! It would look great in-store, would attract consumer attention, and is a very simple, small example of an Adversperience. The retailer said "No" and we had to dumb the whole thing down. They turned the idea down because it was larger than the standard sizing they expected adherence to and was too creative. If they allowed this unconventional thinking for our Adversperience they would have to do it for everyone. Is this not the point of marketing – unconventional thinking?

Retailers will have to change or perish. With the increase in online sales followed by delivery to homes and offices, bricks and mortar retailing in some sectors may actually disappear. I do think in-store sampling/retail-tainment is an effective strategy, but it needs to be re-invented/reset so that it lives up to its original intent.

In his book, *Enchanting a Disenchanted World: Revolutionizing the Means of Consumption* (1999), author George Ritzer describes "retail-tainment" as the "use of ambience, emotion, sound and activity to get customers interested in the merchandise and in a mood to buy."

According to Michael Morrison at the Australian Centre for Retail Studies:

> There is a move towards the concept of 'retailtainment.' This phenomenon, which brings together retailing, entertainment, music and leisure ... Retailers need to look further than the traditional retail store elements such as colour, lighting and visual merchandising to influence buying decisions. The specific atmosphere the retailer creates can, in some cases, be more influential in the decision-making process than the product itself. As goods and services become more of a commodity, it is what a shopper experiences and what atmosphere retailers create that really matters.

Retailers need to be open to new and fresh ideas and fully embrace retail-tainment. More importantly, they need to understand that retail-tainment is a "channel" for our Adversperiences!

And in the case where brands feel the limits or restrictions of "traditional retail," they are taking matters into their own hands – aka Pop-Up Retail. Simply this is when a brand fulfills not only an Adversperience but also invites the consumer to purchase the product. When brands first started to sell direct, versus just through traditional distribution channels, there was quite a stir; today it is becoming more and more commonplace. And in the spirit of disruption and distraction, tradition needs to evolve. Bring on Adversperience! Everywhere!

Chapter 10

It's Not All Fun and Games

B2B Versus B2C

"Can't you give me brains?" asked the Scarecrow.

"You don't need them. You are learning something every day.
A baby has brains, but it doesn't know much. Experience is the
only thing that brings knowledge, and the longer you are on earth
the more experience you are sure to get."

*T*he quote from *The Wizard of Oz* that kicks off this chapter is not only a lesson for life, it is also a key principle that B2B folks live by. B2B folks think, analyze, and listen more than they talk. Then they talk to a few very targeted people. Their conversations are concise and specific. B2B brands and their corresponding marketing and sales teams live and die by their product, industry knowledge, and relationships.

Ask any successful business person what their key to success is and they will say relationships. Relationships propel us – personally and professionally. In business we understand the value, the importance of a customer – likely because it is measured in thousands of dollars. Consumer brand marketers need to equally value their customers – their circles of influence, their word of mouth, and the lifetime value of their loyalty – they all add up to thousands.

What is B2B and why do big corporations spend so much time, effort, and money on Adversperiences – they have been doing them for years? They get the value and they invest the money.

The Research

B2B folks measure – *I love that!* They invest in research to evaluate acquisition, trial, engagement, the list goes on and on and on. They invest in the research to ensure that their engagement with the target is bang on! So it speaks volumes when they invest in Experiential

Marketing – they know it works. Below are some industry insights from EMI Online Research (2008), highlighting the following facts about the B2B side of Experiential Marketing.

- 34% said event marketing gives the highest ROI compared with the next closest (24% for Web advertising).

- 70% measure traffic, 67% measure qualified leads, and 59% followed increased sales.

- The average closure cycle from event to contract signing was 3.8 months for 59% of respondents, with 11% closing the deal within an average of 3.2 weeks.

More research from Red 7 Media also outlines how both attendees and exhibitors at B2B events are quite different from their B2C counterparts.

- 92% of attendees attend events to see new products; their #1 reason for attending.

- 49% of exhibitors say that "launching new products or services" is a main part of their event strategy and goals.

Exhibit 10.1
Why Attendees Go to Business Events

	%
See new products	92%
Keep up to date on industry trends, issues	78%
See many companies at one time	75%
See existing suppliers	67%
See specific companies and products	67%
Network	65%
Create strengthen relationships, partnerships	60%
See products "in-person" first reviewed online	57%
Get technical information, specifications	52%
Attend seminars and workshops	41%

Source: EMI/Mosaic EventTrack 2013

B2B and B2C – What's the Difference?

What's so different about the B2B Experiential Marketing world compared with B2C?

1. **It's Slower:** B2C is defined by speed. The "new and improved" anything or the "next generation" smart phone are designed to create consumer excitement, prompt interest, and ultimately sales. Blackberry (*sorry*), by that measure, is characterized as the ultimate B2B product. Decidedly not flashy, with longer gaps between those next generations, and the not-so exciting feature of e-mail platform security as its main selling point. B2B customers take longer to decide, so Experiential Marketing (*insert* Adversperiential) may serve as an introductory and lead-generating vehicle more so than a deal closer.

2. **Sizzle is Nice; Beef is Better:** The razz-ma-taz that works in the consumer realm does not typically close the deal in the B2B world. In other words, killer displays and great graphics may attract the B2B audience, but only technical and evidence-based facts and specifics will close the sale at the end of the day.

3. **The B2B Audience is a Company, Not a Person:** It may sound obvious, but unless the buyer is a sole proprietor, a B2B sale will involve a number of people. Again, that means a less spontaneous buyer who will be moved by facts and logic more so than an exciting presentation.

4. **The B2C Customer is an Individual, Master of their Domain:** B2B customers represent their company. Others affect, and are affected by, purchasing decisions. Buyer's remorse after buying a soda is totally different than buyer's remorse after buying the wrong machine component for one's plant. With more at stake, B2B advertising must deliver more precise information.

5. **Small Print is the Star:** The stuff that most marketers don't have time or energy to tout in consumer advertising, like mileage, depreciation, and resale value, in the case of autos, is gold to the B2B customer. Any effective B2B Experiential Marketing is going to be chock full of reassuring facts and figures.

6. **Your Buyers have Other Interests:** B2B customers attending your Experiential event may not be interested in your product or service; they might just be there to network.

(Source: "Six Ways B2B and B2C Will Always Differ" at http://www.godfrey.com/How-We-Think/B2B-Insights-Blog/Advertising/Six-Ways-B2B-and-B2C-Will-Always-Differ.aspx)

In my mind the key difference between B2B and B2C is that B2B is relationship driven and B2C is product driven. This is the reason that in the B2C world we look to other sources to create emotional connections such as causes, sponsorships, endorsements and the reason that the focus in so many campaigns today is on storytelling. All these techniques are attempts to build relationships with the target audiences on mass.

For the B2B marketplace, the target group is small, up close, and personal, while the B2C is large, spread across entire countries or continents. Are we realistic when we expect that a TV ad will be seen and interpreted the same by a person in Little Rock, Arkansas, and Chicoutimi, Quebec – language barriers aside?

The key difference, however, is that B2B is a much more rationale decision whereas B2C is emotionally charged, hence the importance of branding and the myriad of other layers we add onto the products we market.

All of this reinforces for me the need to execute Adversperiences. They get B2C as up close and personal as you can reasonably get, given finite budgets and resources.

The B2B Adversperience

Tradeshows are B2B Adversperiences! There are months of planning followed by meticulous attention to prospects and current client detail, that includes everything from invites to reminders about personal milestones to bringing up in conversation to appointments during the event to VIP treatment at the event to follow-up notes and meetings – even if there is not current business on the table. A chief marketing officer for an ad agency once told me he courted a client for five years – dinners, joint attendance at conferences and events – at year five they began working together – and several years and no RFPs later, they are still working together. Time, effort, investment, follow-up – all critical factors.

When building B2B Adversperiential plans, the process is very similar to that of B2C, but with three key differences in the execution.

1. **Greater Focus on Areas to Meet, Chat, Lounge:** Often there is coffee, and a place to sit and casually meet, with lots of brochures with key product facts.

2. **Brand Ambassadors Keep the Experience Clean, Neat, and Act as Receptionists/Hosts:** The heavy lifting and critical conversations are all lead by key sales and marketing people from the organization. The conversations at a tradeshow are intense. The details matter so the front line needs to understand the business, the products, the challenges. The ability to engage in critical dialogue and find solutions is the key to building the relationship.

3. **Ongoing Communication:** In whatever form works for the client – e-mail, social media, phone calls – the ongoing conversations will determine if and when a sale will be made. In the case of B2B, a website trumps a Facebook page! While a client will certainly want to know who "likes" you, this is not a thumbs up on a page but rather a detailed phone call with one of your clients sourced via you or LinkedIn!

In the B2B world we all intuitively understand the importance of every interaction. The truth is we need to do the same in the B2C world.

The B2B world often engages their employees first showcasing the latest and greatest to the first and most important sea of ambassadors – their own people. Then they take it to places where their key target clients will gather. And, very importantly, they put their very best people on the front line.

In the B2C world we can take these points into consideration but obviously need to adjust them for scope, scale, and reach. Importantly, we need to structure and design our engagements so that we are as up close and personal as possible and so that they are admission worthy. If, when you step back and evaluate your Adversperience you could easily see yourself and your target consumer paying an admission fee, then you have achieved success. While the yellow brick road may be paved with good intentions, the keys to the gate that unlocks the doors to The Emerald City are priceless. If you take the time and are prepared to pay the price (make your Adversperience admission charge worthy) so too will your target – then everyone wins and the "flood gates" open …

Chapter 11

Speak!

WORD of MOUTH

While Dorothy was looking earnestly into the queer, painted face of the Scarecrow, she was surprised to see one of the eyes slowly wink at her. She thought she must have been mistaken at first, for none of the scarecrows in Kansas ever wink; but presently the figure nodded its head to her in a friendly way. ...

"Good day," said the Scarecrow, in a rather husky voice.

"Did you speak?" asked the girl, in wonder.

We all "speak" with our hands, our eyes, our mouths. Today, however, we converse on so many levels.

At one time, word of mouth spread around a campfire. It was how we passed on learning, wisdom, legacies. Today it spreads like wildfire over electronic devices to millions in seconds. On the one hand, I yearn for the peace of the campfire and, on the other, I am thankful for knowing that I can connect and share life moments with loved ones thousands of miles away in seconds.

Both are genuine and authentic. Both have a time, place, and pace.

Perhaps pace is the key, but the objective is to determine how to amplify word of mouth and social media.

Social Media as Word of Mouth (WOM)

According to WOMMA (Word of Mouth Marketing Association), word of mouth is "any business action that earns a customer recommendation," but in the big world of creative campaigns and engagement techniques, WOM means much more. WOM is about harnessing the power of people to build brand awareness.

Social media refers to the means of interactions among people in which they create, share, and/or exchange information and ideas in virtual communities and networks.

According to me, social media is word of mouth on steroids!

In a previous chapter we identified what happens every 60 seconds in the social media world. It's crazy, and yet, "Only 7 percent of word of mouth happens online," said Jonah Berger, a marketing professional at the Wharton business school at the University of Pennsylvania. "Marketers are always chasing the shiniest new toys and jumping on the bandwagon, but it's important to take a step back and think about the strategy." (Source: *The Globe and Mail*, August 16, 2013)

Key Differences

Live word of mouth is one thing; social/digital word of mouth is an entirely different beast for a few key reasons.

- **Live WOM has a Point of Reference:** You know the person, so their credentials play a role in the value you place on their feedback.

- **Live WOM Spreads to a "Small Circle:"** You tell family and friends, typically less than 25 to 50 people. Digital/social word of mouth can spread to thousands in seconds.

- **Live WOM Spreads, with Potential to Evolve Consistently and Inconsistently:** We rarely tell the same story with the same detail twice and when we share a story that someone told us (hearsay), it is, of course, told with our filter. In the digital/social world there is a cut and paste, a forwarding, or a "re-tweet" option so the details are in their exact state from the original source as they are passed on.

WOM as Part of an Adversperience

Word of mouth – live or online – is *critical* to building a brand. We all understand that. Key to this is, of course, ensuring the "right" conversation is happening hence the focus on making certain your products deliver and your marketing communications and Adversperience communicates the right messages, resonates, and is relevant. I think every chapter in this book has preached this gospel. Assuming you activate an Adversperiential, how do you ensure your brand maintains a healthy "social voice?" And, how do you track it?

Let's begin with doing it right.

The Foundation

Paul Jankowski, Chief Strategist at Access Brand Strategies, a brand strategy/consumer engagement agency in Nashville, TN, authored an article in Forbes online, "4 Tactics to BuildYour Word of Mouth."

- **Target Influencers** – Make sure you are speaking to leaders and influencers in your space. These can be journalists, public figures, bloggers, or even trend-setting fans. The age of Social Media has given everyone the power to broadcast their opinions and some bloggers and YouTube sensations have amassed strong followings. It is a good idea to make a target list of influencers that appeal to your key demographic and make sure that they know about what you do. This does not mean badger them with calls and emails – but rather take the time to learn about them and why they are influential, then open up a dialogue by engaging with their content in ways that are relevant to your brand.

- **Build a Close Knit Social Media Community** – The easiest way to directly communicate with your audience is to engage with them via social platforms. Social Media has exploded in recent years, and a study conducted by Pew Research Centers in 2012 found that 65% of internet users use social media. Of users on Facebook, 58% liked a brand page in 2011 and 41% shared content about that brand on their wall. Sharing content with friends online is even more valuable as verbal word of mouth.

- **Be a Thought Leader:** – Not only do you want to target the influencers in your space...You want to be one! Figure out what makes you and your business unique, and tell people about it. This can (and should) be communicated on your website, but also figure out where to best reach your target audience. This might be on social media, but maybe it is through speaking at a conference or starting a blog. Figure out the medium that best supports your ideas and develop a strategy to grow your presence there.

- **ALWAYS be honest** – The success of Word of Mouth marketing depends on customer's trust of the brand. You have to earn enough merit to become a worthy topic of conversation. You can do this with an exceptional product and by maintaining integrity across online platforms (your website, social media, and mobile).

WOM and Adversperience

While Paul provides solid principles for building a strong foundation to grow your word of mouth, let me suggest how this can be applied to an Adversperience.

1. **Begin with Your Most Important Stakeholders:** Share with your employees first, then key distribution channels, and finally key influencers in the social world – online and off. Literally carve out the circles of influence and optimize the ripple effect. As an aside I am always surprised when companies don't launch to their own employees first. It is amazing for motivation but it is also a great place to build word of mouth momentum because these people are engaged, enlightened, and will (hopefully) share not only positively but with credibility and knowledge.

2. **Build a Tracking System/Agree to Measurement:** Said with the greatest of respect, thousands of followers and thousands of likes does not necessarily equate to an engaged and loyal sea of ambassadors. Define who you want to talk to. Are you reaching them? See what they are saying. Evaluate if they are staying connected. Ensure through your own efforts that you have built in a way to keep them loyal. Very simplistically think of this almost the way you would an employee retention strategy – identification, retention, evaluation, development. An Adversperience provides the perfect opportunity to

gain one-on-one information about anyone and everyone who engages with your brand. *Use it!* Build this in from the start. It is the power of an Adversperience and the reason its ROI is and always will be the highest of anything you do and trackable.

3. **Authentically Maintain and Leverage Conversations:** A brand's "social voice" is the same as your own. When you engage so too does your circle. Shut off (metaphorically) your phone and no one calls! With TV, radio, print, outdoor there is a push message. With online there is the hope that the target will click and a conversation will begin, assuming the target has seen your ad. How many dotcom pages are there in the world? Search engine optimization and targeting help but still there are millions and millions of pages. An Adversperience on the other hand delivers a "qualified target." They are engaged and want to be engaged. They are interested and want to know about your brand so take the time, ask a few questions, and then respectfully and authentically keep the dialogue healthy and alive.

Tracking Word of Mouth

Having shared the principles of how and what to do the next key is to track. Tracking social voice and its impact is relatively new, as is optimizing it, but for those who have taken the time the value is unreal! Speaking to value, McKinsey & Company has identified ten ways to measure word of mouth. They have also identified that word of mouth is the primary factor behind 20-50% of all purchasing decisions. Word of mouth can be dissected to understand exactly what makes it effective and its impact can be measured using what we call "word of mouth equity" – an index of a brand's power to generate messages that influence the consumer's decision to purchase.

McKinsey also stated that Experiential word of mouth is the most common and powerful form, typically accounting for 50-80% of word of mouth activity in any given product category. Here are the key drivers. (Source: *McKinsey Quarterly*, April 2010, "A New Way to Measure Word-of-Mouth Marketing")

1. **What's Said:** The content of a message must address important product or service features if it is to influence consumer decisions. Marketers tend to build campaigns around emotional positioning, yet we found that consumers actually tend to talk – and generate buzz – about functional messages.

2. **The Identity of the Person who Sends the Message:** The receiver must trust the sender and believe that he or she really knows the product or service in question. Eight to nine percent of consumers are those we call "influential" and their common factor is trust and competence. Influentials typically generate three times more word of mouth messages than non-influentials do and each message has four times more impact on a recipient's purchasing decision. About 1% of these people are digitally influential – most notably bloggers – with disproportionate power.

3. **The Environment where Word of Mouth Circulates:**
This is crucial to the power of messages. Typically
messages passed within tight, trusted networks have
less reach but greater impact than those circulated
through dispersed communities – in part usually
because there's a high correlation between people
whose opinions we trust and the members of networks
we most value. That's why old-fashioned kitchen
table recommendations and their online equivalents
remain so important. After all, a person with 400
friends on Facebook may happily ignore the advice
of 290 of them. It's the small close-knit network of
friends that has the most real influence.

As I was sitting proofing this chapter I flipped through
a magazine on my desk (*yes, the hard copy – I like the tactile
experience!*). The article was about twitter and how a new
generation of TV viewers is tuning out ads to tweet. The
example provided was that of Kanye West's hijacking of
Taylor Swift's acceptance speech at the 2009 MTV Video
Music Awards." In the article, Jesse Brown (Toronto Life,
November 2013) reminded us that,

> Kanye may have permanently upset the balance between
> television and the Internet. The online reaction to the
> incident was instant and global. Viewers tweeted about the
> moment during the ad breaks. It might have been the birth
> of what is now known as the 'second-screen' experience,
> wherein a new generation of TV viewers tune out commer-
> cials, engaging instead with friends through phones, tablets
> and laptops. In the days that followed, the YouTube clip
> alone was viewed more than 20 million times ...

The number of people participating in the social media aftershock of the moment was larger than the audience for the awards broadcast itself.

At this point, I feel like the point on the effectiveness/power/impact of social media is more than proven. That said what does it mean to you as a marketer? When and where does it apply to your brand?

Harbinger and Ipsos conducted a North American study on the social influence of women. (Source: 2010 Harbinger, "Women and Word-of-Mouth" study at *www.harbingerideas.com*). Women are using a combination of offline and online forms of word of mouth to seek and spread the word on products and services. The key reasons for sharing were a "good personal experience – 86%" or a "bad personal experience – 80%." There is lots more juicy info so check it out online at *harbingerideas.com*. My point is that as a brand marketer you need to understand why, when, and how consumers will share about your brand and try to steer the conversation positively to the best of your ability. Very similar to managing your own reputation, you need to consistently and persistently manage your brand's persona.

The beauty of an Adversperience is that it is based in human interaction and conversation so the sharing of brand information and knowledge is personal and two way so that as a question, comment, or concern is raised it can be addressed immediately. Assuming we have executed a great Adversperience, the intent is to get the target, in the short term, to try the product/service and in the long term grow and maintain the "love" so that they share via word of mouth through their online and offline social networks. The hope is that the cyclone is now off in the distance and instead we (and our brands) are riding the wave as the "flood gates" into The Emerald City open. We are here; we have arrived!

Never doubt that a small group of
thoughtful, committed citizens can
change the world; indeed, it's the
only thing that ever has.

Margaret Mead

Chapter 12

The Emerald City of Oz

The EMERALD CITY of ADVERSPERIENCE

"That must be the Emerald City," said Dorothy.

As they walked on, the green glow became brighter and brighter, and it seemed that at last they were nearing the end of their travels. Yet is was afternoon before they came to the great wall that surrounded the City. It was high and thick and of a bright green color.

...

"... since you demand to see the Great Oz I must take you to his Palace. But first you must put on the spectacles."

"Why?" asked Dorothy.

"Because if you did not wear spectacles the brightness and glory of the Emerald City would blind you. Even those who live in the City must wear spectacles night and day. ..."

"Even with eyes protected by the green spectacles, Dorothy and her friends were at first dazzled by the brilliancy of the wonderful City."

Just as all fairy tales draw to a close with "and they lived happily ever after," so too does this one. With Dorothy safely back in Kansas we are knee deep sifting through brand plans, research, briefs, and ideas. Firmly grounded in the real world, we must all embrace that there is actually no firm ground. The cyclone and pace of rapid change is here to stay and likely even accelerate. For all of us adrenaline junkies – bring it! No need to fear what is coming around the corner – grab hold and intelligently react. In the words of L. Frank Baum, author of *The Wizard of Oz,* "Never give up. No one knows what's going to happen next."

In fairness only the fittest, fastest, and smartest will survive because that is what it is going to take. The Oreo social media leverage of the lights going out at the 2013 Superbowl is a perfect example. Response needs to be right and fast; it needs to be seconds and minutes not weeks; and smart people need to be empowered to work the front lines. This certainly changes the way we think, organize, and structure, but that is and will be the cost of being in business. We need to "be the target" we are seeking. We need to have the self-awareness to know what surprises and delights us and realize that we are someone's target, maybe even our own – and that we must ensure the brands we steward surprise and delight – every minute of every day. It is incumbent upon all of us to keep the connection and conversation going and growing while the world continues to ebb and flow and shift and shake all around us.

As I adjust my green spectacles, here are some thoughts from a practical, crystal ball-lacking, simple mind, abeit with some witch-like eccentricities and wizardly wiles.

The more things change, the more things remain the same. Disruption, distraction, convergence are the natural order of things, and will continue to be so, offset by the basic human need for live connection that touches all the senses with extra attention to head and heart.

As I type, the most talked about TV show finale of 2013 was *Breaking Bad*'s satisfying ending, with Walter White meeting his fate along with a host of bad guys. That last episode was watched by 10.3 million viewers. Not too bad, *but* (*and I know I am dating myself*) the final episode of *MASH* drew more than 121 million viewers in 1983, or ten times the audience *Breaking Bad* managed.

I don't really watch TV. I have dialed down listening to the radio because there is too much noise/chatter and they play the same loop of songs over and over and over! My iPod and laptop are filled with music and play-lists that ensure I can dance or chill. The odd billboard catches my attention but I usually drive and talk on the phone or listen to an audio book so I am focused on driving and listening. For news I turn to some key social media and online sites. I *love* magazines and books and prefer the real physical printed copies versus online. I love tearing out pictures and keeping them for inspiration. That said, I watched my son read an online magazine and it changed my perspective. The reading became an experience as he flipped from an article to a deeper and deeper dive by connecting to links and ideas embedded in the article. Advertisers need to get this! This too is Adversperience.

I stated this at the beginning and I will say it again – Adversperience is the convergence of advertising and experiential marketing. Brands need to engage their target on a multi-sensory level and provide some theater and interest ... an Adversperience! I don't think I am much different than most of you – from 4-84 year olds we are all scrolling iPads – hopefully consuming different info but scrolling nonetheless.

My greatest tools are my iPhone, BlackBerry, laptop, and journal that I take *everywhere*. My peers and family can attest – *everywhere*! And when reduced to one piece it's my iPhone – substitute in your brand of choice and you get my point.

As we accelerate through the next five to ten years it goes without saying that our technology will evolve. I think computers will be something that when shutdown will be the size of our smart phones but will easily unfold/project to be the size of our choice – we will actually decide. At first keyboards and screens will physically fold or roll out (we are already seeing this) but soon they will be projections and as long as we have a surface we will be good to go.

The bottom line is that technology will continue to surprise and delight us and I think most of us feel we don't fully optimize what we have, yet we crave the newer version – funny!

What's coming in the media world? Not sure we will ever use the words "mass media" again. I'm not sure I even know what it means anymore. "TV," though I think I should type "on-screen," advertising for mega events like the Super Bowl, Olympics, live music festivals, and concerts will continue to be noteworthy, justified because they are events that engage global audiences. Otherwise, media is and will continue to be completely redefined. We will have "on screen," "sound," "touch." It will be defined by the sense it touches, not by the medium. "The message will be the medium," to paraphrase Marshall McLuhan.

McLuhan's original statement, "The message is the medium," was made in 1964. And today it rings equally true. "McLuhan proposed that a medium itself, not the content it carries, should be the focus of study. He said that a medium affects the society in which it plays a role not only by the content delivered over the medium, but also by the characteristics of the medium itself."

To build on McLuhan's point, I think that while the means by which we engage with brands will change, how we absorb and engage will not. Technology is evolving but as humans we still have two eyes, two ears, one nose, one mouth, ... you get the point. While some things will most certainly change (at the speed of sound), some things will remain very much the same. There I said it again.

Some basic underlying principles for connecting to humans will forever drive our engagement. The return to one to one, the need to share, look each other in the eye will continue to be the foundation for everything and hence the need to embrace an Adversperiential model for marketing brands.

In the world of consumables, expect the "mindless" proliferation of product extensions to gain a few more ticks of market share to stop. Thanks to real conversations with target consumers companies will hear exactly what is needed and will stop the insanity of production ad nauseum. (To my point in an earlier chapter do we really need eight varieties of eggs?) In some cases mass proliferation will be replaced by mass customization. A prime example is running shoes. This trend has already begun. You can select materials, designs, hit order and your shoes will be sent to your door. Where appropriate and within certain guidelines, mass customization will grow. In the case of eggs, however, I think we will be reminded that life can be simpler, if the creative lead at my agency is any indication. The backyard of his city home now features a chicken coup, balanced however by his insatiable hunger for the latest technology! Latest and greatest balanced with simpler times – the ultimate challenge of all marketers.

The trend (more of a save the earth reality) towards simplifying life and protecting the environment will force consumers and companies to get real about what we all really need.

Expect 3-D printing to continue to evolve to the point that replication is to the exact detail. It is doubtful that most people will have 3-D printers in their homes, churning out custom products like *Star Trek* replicators, but there will come a day when we design a product on our computer and transfer the files online to an "outputter" and then either go pick it up or have it shipped a few hours or days later depending on the complexity.

Some traditional retail will be killed by Amazon or its online successors. Others will evolve their environments to enhance the experience, hence the reason so many bookstores now have coffee shops with great music playing in the background. Many of us still like and need the tactile shopping experience, so retailers will need to ensure their offerings are unique enough to draw us in and, once inside, the experience will be entertaining so that we linger and spend some money as opposed to evaluating and purchasing online.

Online shopping will continue to grow, especially in areas where the price advantage or the commoditization of the product make it okay to wait a day or more before we receive it. In the instances where we need immediate gratification like clothes, it will continue to be tough to wait a day or more (in my opinion).

Social media and media in general will continue to grow exponentially but we will more selectively choose our circles. We will test new circles and technology, keep what fits, and discard the rest. As for media, we will use filters from the likes of Google and search for areas of interest and then tune in or out. Watch Google – I think they are going to take over the world!

What Does All this Mean for Adversperience?

Adversperience will be the winner at the end of the day. It is the Emerald City. Increasingly, people will leave their homes and their computers because they want to "humanly" interact. We need to engage with each other to enrich our lives and so too will brands in order to get our attention.

Agencies will become Adversperiential hot beds of creativity, because the only way to reach the consumer will be through a one-to-one interaction. The pressure will be do it very, *very* well. But that is the fun brain hurt part!

There is a famous expression, "Actions speak louder than words." This reigns true regardless of time, space, the way we live, and the business of brands. Brands need to be sensory beings connecting on multiple levels with their target. As a result, agencies will need to remodel. Brand campaigns will focus on integrating touchpoints and ensuring a common "voice/thread" not mediums or competencies. Agencies will therefore become more strategic, more aware of critical consumer insights and triggers. Development of all the ways that a consumer dates, courts, introduces to family and friends, marries, and re-evaluates a brand will need to be mapped – all at the speed of sound. Just as every person and every brand has a story, we will draw people into our story by ensuring it is relevant, resonates, and is compelling, very similar to the first glance that turns into a kiss.

Examples of true Adversperiential campaigns are being created as I type. In my opinion, the best so far is Samsung's recent new launch of the Galaxy S4. Pre-launch hype that it was coming attracted loyal and new users. A live physical installation showcased a projection line-up with 12,000 avatars appearing very real who represented consumers. The12,000 representative avatars moved up the line the more they shared the new features of the phone. Over 3,000,000 tweets, 15,000,000 impressions, and a 12% increase in market share and the conversation continues.

Examples of Adversperiential campaigns are very much in the works. Please share them with us and the world at *adverseperience.com.*

What Is the "Next Big Thing?" What Does the Future Hold ... Who Knows?

With my green spectacles sitting firmly on the bridge of my nose, I hope I have given you a sense of how we have gotten to this place in time and what the future holds. I still shudder a bit and feel the tail winds from the cyclone circling in the distance but I am quickly reminded to pause and return to the discipline of moving, step by step, along the yellow brick road to the Wizard of Oz landing in the Emerald City of my design, an Adversperiental mecca – a new marketing paradigm, an Adversperiential paradigm upon which to build extraordinary brands.

It's funny the road seems to keep twisting and turning, so many thoughts, so many conversations, so many ideas, so much to do, and think and see … I love it!

Hooting, hollering, and holding hands with my dream team and my colleagues, we are heading back into the fairy tale world where our creative juices flow and the yellow brick road will provide a framework. Wizards of our own desire in the Emerald City of Adversperience … care to join us?!

Join the Adversperiential Revolution!

"The Silver Shoes," said the Good Witch, "have wonderful powers. And one of the most curious things about them is that they can carry you to any place in the world in three steps, and each step will be made in the wink of an eye. All you have to do is to knock the heels together three times and command the shoes to carry you wherever you wish to go."

In the words of L. Frank Baum, "Everything has to come to an end, sometime."

At *adversperience.com* the conversation is just beginning – join in!